THE LIFE AND ART OF INA D.D. UHTHOFF

The Unheralded Artists of BC — 5

THE LIFE AND ART OF
INA D.D. UHTHOFF

CHRISTINA JOHNSON-DEAN

INTRODUCTION BY PAT MARTIN BATES

MOTHER TONGUE PUBLISHING LIMITED
Salt Spring Island, B.C.
Canada

Library and Archives Canada Cataloguing in Publication

Johnson-Dean, Christina B., 1944–
          The life and art of Ina D.D. Uhthoff / Christina Johnson-Dean ; introduction by Pat Martin Bates.

(Unheralded Artists of BC)

Includes index.

ISBN 978–1–896949–13–0

          1. Uhthoff, Ina D. D. 2. Uhthoff, Ina D. D.—Criticism and interpretation. 3. Painters—British Columbia—Biography. 4. Painting, Canadian—British Columbia—20th century. I. Uhthoff, Ina D. D. II. Title. III. Series: Unheralded artists of BC

ND249.U47J64 2012   759.11   C2012–901376–5

PREVIOUS SPREAD—
Untitled (Early self portrait of Ina), n.d.
pencil on paper
6½" x 5"
MICHAEL UHTHOFF COLLECTION
PHOTO BY JANET DWYER

› *Untitled* (Mt Baker from Cattle Point)
n.d., watercolour
10½" x 13¾"
JOHNSON-DEAN PRIVATE COLLECTION
PHOTO BY AUTHOR

Book design, layout and typesetting by Jan Westendorp
Typeset in Whitman—a typeface designed by Kent Lew—and URW Grotesk, designed by Hermann Zapf. Cover type also includes Alexander Quill, designed by Jim Rimmer.

All efforts have been made to locate copyright holders of source material wherever possible.

Printed and bound in Canada by Friesens
Printed on chlorine-free paper; inside pages are 10% PCW

Mother Tongue Publishing gratefully acknowledges the support of the Canada Council for the Arts, which last year invested $20.1 million in writing and publishing throughout Canada; and the assistance of the Province of British Columbia through the B.C. Arts Council.

Nous remercions de son soutien le Conseil des Arts du Canada, qui a investi 20,1 millions de dollars l'an dernier dans les lettres et l'édition à travers le Canada.

Published by:

Mother Tongue Publishing Limited
290 Fulford-Ganges Road
Salt Spring Island, B.C. V8K 2K6
Canada
phone: 250–537–4155   fax: 250–537–4725

www.mothertonguepublishing.com

Represented in Canada by the Literary Press Group and distributed by LitDistCo in North America

To my sister, Nelia Johnson, with whom I've enjoyed
a lifetime of stories, ideas, and books

Contents

‹ *Mount Temple*, 20th century
oil on canvas, 12½" x 9¼"
IMAGE #M964.1.118, COURTESY
OF THE UNIVERSITY OF VICTORIA
ART COLLECTIONS, LEGACY ART
GALLERY, UNIVERSITY OF VICTORIA ART
COLLECTIONS PHOTO

INTRODUCTION

"Let the beauty of what you love be what you do"
—Rumi

The waves were wild that morning in 1964 when the phone rang. A beautiful voice said, "My name is Ina Uhthoff. Would you care to have tea with me this afternoon. Tony Emery, Colin Graham and Gwladys Downes mentioned we should meet." I was thrilled for I knew of this remarkable artist from her outstanding exhibition, April 1962. I see her still, smiling in the Constance Avenue doorway. They say one soul recognizes another, and so it was. Ina resonated with a kind of shine, her brown eyes warm with the light of the Seeker after Truth in the Arts. Seemingly taller than she actually was, slim and trim with lovely legs, she was quite elegant. I remember her expressive hands and only now realize Ina would have been in her 70s, almost 40 years between us. She reminded me of my Bell relatives, those neat little ladies with questioning eyes. We sat in her living room, drinking tea and eating oatcakes, which I love. There were small paintings on the walls by friends, for in those days artists exchanged works. One of Ina's artworks was cubistic, akin to abstract expressionism. Yet not. She seemed to be ahead of her time. Although Ina had not travelled as widely as other artists, she had great memories of Scotland and England. "To see Derbyshire you must walk," she said, "use the footpaths beside the streams, walk through the meadows of the deep grasses." She understood Nature and knew the joy of mountain tops. Sometimes in our many talks, we would say, wouldn't you love to go to the top of something! And how she loved the water; "The Pull," Ina would say. The sea calls us and the mourning seagulls echo. I then sang her a sad seagull song my grandmother sang to me. And yes, I did bring a book of Scottish songs, in English and Gallic, to another visit, and she knew quite a few. Perhaps she was a singer as well.

We talked about everything. The unhappiness of losing a father at a young age and trying not to show it. The joy of teaching. The classical training: all those plaster busts! How refreshing to speak about the training and our teachers, she having studied at the great Glasgow School of Art. Another thing we had in common was not dating or signing our works although pushing students to do so! We laughed a lot over what our children did as preschoolers. She had a great wit.

The 60s were a time of creativity in all the arts, and Ina was always in the fore-front. We conversed about artists, not only Canadian, but the greats like Chagall whose works Ina interpreted in a mystical fashion, intrigued that, as a student, I had actually met him in 1957. Ina explained Kathleen Maltwood's theories to me, King Arthur's seat and the Zodiac. We felt Esquimalt must be on one of those lay lines and was the place to start an art school. Ina was the only artist with intaglio fine art training, etching, engraving, mezzotint, aquatint. She agreed that there was a need for such graphic work and that there were no studio spaces for young artists with limited means. In 1967, when the Department of National Defense rented me the old brick buildings vacated by the Maritime Museum for $100 a year, we were thrilled with the potential. Under the umbrella Creative Centres Organization (we hoped to acquire other derelict buildings), they became the Signal Hill Creative Centre, rent-ing studios for $15 a month to pay for heating. I opened Signal Hill Print Workshop in my studio and a gallery called The Purple Door Is Contagious. Ina gave me not only encouragement but very, very good advice.

Ina was more help and inspiration to me than I knew, especially now as I am of that certain age when women artists feel "there is no one out there," even though many friends and former students still come calling. The body becomes a cage, and one cannot drive to watch the sea, the sea, the sea. When Ina, at the end of this book, indicates she is lonely that no one comes, I think of those same words coming from Emily Carr in Edythe Hembroff-Schleicher's book[1]: "I'm at the end of a long dark cor-ridor where no one comes...." We all want someone of like spirit to talk with—about a tackier ink, a softer paper and what do you really think of Rodin?

Yes, my friend Ina was a Shaper and Image Maker, a Giver of Form who under-stood the universal language that everyone understands—the Language of Enthusiasm with things accomplished with Love and Purpose and as part of some-thing believed in and desired—an artist to salute with fond affection.

PAT MARTIN BATES
VICTORIA, 2012

ONE

Scottish Start

NA D.D. UHTHOFF, an expert fly fisher as well as an accomplished artist, teacher, administrator and writer, knew how to balance being open and fluid while applying discipline, careful detail, hard work and a critical eye. She negotiated the traditional waters of British Columbia's artistically staid capital city, Victoria, while experimenting, shepherding and bringing to the fore new waves in a provincial art world of the mid-1900s. Ina admirably maintained both a steady livelihood as a single parent of two and a highly respected reputation, while engaging fully in a career through the controversial rapids of twentieth-century aesthetic tastes and movements.

Named after her mother, Ina was born Jemima Duncan Dewar Campbell on December 5, 1889 at Ericht Bank Villa, near Kirn, Argyle County, District of Dunoon, Scotland.[1] A family photo of her birthplace shows a sailboat in front of this large waterfront residence. Located on the mouth of the Clyde River, west

Gordon Street, Glasgow
n.d., etching, 14" x 9½"
JOY UHTHOFF/NANCY
WHITE COLLECTION
PHOTO BY NANCY WHITE

Untitled, 1912, sepia
drawing, 13¾" x 14½"
FIONA HERT COLLECTION
PHOTO BY MICHAEL A. COOK

› Diploma from Glasgow
School of Art for Ina
Campbell, 1912
MICHAEL UHTHOFF
COLLECTION
PHOTO BY JANET DWYER

of the large shipbuilding and trading city of Glasgow, the family home was across
the waters from Greenock, the early home of her father, John Blackwell Campbell, a
Commission Agent (supplying shipyards).

On March 13, 1870, John Campbell, who was from a large Catholic family, married Jemima Dewar, also from a "Scots family,"[2] in Glasgow. Alec, their first born,
was followed by three daughters, Kate, Lillian (Lily) and Edith (Edie)—who preceded
Jemima (nicknamed Ina, the name she used all her life), their fifth child.[3] A younger
brother, John, died in infancy. The family was well-to-do and provided a sheltered
upbringing for their children. As was common in this era, girls of her class in Great
Britain were often privately educated. There is no record about her early education,
but traditionally, love of the outdoors and nature were encouraged, along with litera-

Untitled (Young Woman with Book), n.d., ink and watercolour, 7¼" x 5¼"
FIONA HERT COLLECTION

ture, arts and the natural sciences. Drawing and painting were common pastimes.

Alec, the oldest sibling, taught his adventurous youngest sister some of her fly-fishing skills. "She was very, very attached to her brother… who was a great outdoorsman… and a great fisherman… she used to spend a great deal of her girlhood days with him, flashing around on the moors… and trying to catch fish."[4] Ina also had considerable affection for her father, who died when she was young, which was probably why Ina was so close to her brother. The family cherished a treasured trophy cup that John Campbell had won as a yachtsman.[5]

In 1905, Ina, a tall attractive young woman with short dark wavy hair and brown eyes, enrolled in the Glasgow School of Art (GSA), which had started in 1845 as the Glasgow Government School of Design. The Campbells were then living in Glasgow at 2 St. James Terrace, Hillhead.[6] On an upward swing, the school had opened a new building on Renfrew Street in 1899, designed inside and out by the influential Charles Rennie Mackintosh. Known for his work as an architect, designer, watercolourist and sculptor, Mackintosh and his artist wife, Margaret MacDonald (whom he had met at the GSA), had a lasting impact on the city as proponents of the Arts and Crafts and art nouveau movements, bringing forth an appreciation of uncluttered, well-crafted work, based on early European as well as Japanese aesthetics. While Ina was in attendance, the second half of the building was completed in 1909 and still serves as the nucleus for an art school with a much larger student population and well-established reputation. In these formative years of her artistic development, Ina was in the centre of a thriving art community, based on an appreciation of sound training and understanding of the past, yet pushing the borders of "modern" in the early 1900s.

At the GSA, Ina started with afternoon classes; later she was listed as a day student. During her first two years, she was enrolled in the Lower Course. She took Drawing and Painting as well as Life classes from professors David Forrester Wilson, William Edward Frank Britten, Paul Artot and Maurice Greiffenhagen.[7] The latter was clearly the one she credited with her most valuable learning, often listing him in her credentials. She wrote later:

I had a grand time there [at the GSA]. Maurice Greiffenhagen, R.A. was [the] professor in Life class. A great draftsman and illustrator, he was more of a friend than a teacher… his example was of lasting value in the years that followed.[8]

Though times and places are unclear, Ina was also a student of R. Auering Bell for Decorative Design and Composition, Susan Crawford (A.R.E.[9]) for Etching, Johann Keller for Modelling[10] and Fra H. Newbury.[11] Ina had difficulty reconciling "her love of divertissements with the stern demands of the teaching studio," and between studies she would meet her friends at the Mackintosh tea rooms; acceptable places for young women to be seen in public. After attending the GSA for six years, Ina was awarded a Diploma in 1912, but was officially enrolled until 1913. Though the diploma shows that the school featured drawing, painting, architecture, modelling, design and decoration, Ina noted that her diploma was for painting. While there, she was continually exhibiting, included in group shows at the Royal Glasgow Institute of Fine Arts in 1911, 1912 and 1913 and with the Royal Scottish Academy in 1912.[12] Ina rarely dated her work, but etchings and ink drawings of Glasgow and fashionable women are likely from these earlier years.[13] By 24, Ina Uhthoff had established herself as an artist.

◂ *Untitled*, 1912, graphite 14" x 10", NANCY WHITE COLLECTION
PHOTO BY NANCY WHITE

◂ *Untitled*, n.d., etching, 11¼" x 8 ½", MICHAEL UHTHOFF COLLECTION
PHOTO BY JANET DWYER

TWO

Western Canada Adventure

IN 1913, INA EMBARKED on an adventurous post-graduation trip across the seas to Canada to visit the Frasers a friend and her husband, who had gone to Canada for the "simple life." They had lived on Edinburgh's Douglas Crescent, which Ina described as "quite the most snooty district with titled clientele and five or six story houses," before emigrating to remote British Columbia.[1] Their home, Ledlanet Ranch, Crawford Bay, on the eastern shore of Kootenay Lake, was Ina's destination.[2] A rustic settlement in Creston Valley, named after a trapper and gold prospector, it was originally a supply store for steamboats plying Kootenay Lake in the early nineteenth century. It was more than a day's trip east of Vancouver, then a developing coastal town, much smaller than the complex Scottish cities they had left behind.

‹ *Untitled,* n.d., watercolour
6¾" x 10", MICHAEL
UHTHOFF COLLECTION
PHOTO BY JANET DWYER

Hastings Street, circa 1914, ink on paper 7" x 4½", COLLECTION OF THE VANCOUVER ART GALLERY, ACQUISITION FUND, VAG 92.29.1

Ina sailed "deck cabin" on the *Empress of Britain*. She recalled gardenias at her dinner plate, as well as royalty at the next table. From Quebec, she took the train across Canada and then in B.C. a passenger sternwheeler, arriving at Crawford Bay near Nelson "in fragile city shoes" in December, snow piled up past her ankles. Ina sat on cold wooden planks for five or six miles as a wagon and a team of horses jolted along roads that were "merely sketched in."

Vancouver from Kitsilano, circa 1914 ink on paper, 4½" x 7" COLLECTION OF THE VANCOUVER ART GALLERY, REPRODUCED FROM JOHN UHTHOFF'S SLIDES, JOY/ MICHAEL UHTHOFF PRIVATE COLLECTION, DIGITALLY RESTORED BY JANET DWYER

> That night I cried myself to sleep as I was distinctly a city girl and had been accustomed to all the comforts. I thought I had reached the end of the world, but I soon found that these appearances fooled me.[3]

At Ledlanet Ranch, the only luxury was the grand piano; the family rugs, silver and linen had been left behind in Edinburgh. It must have been quite a time of adjustment. They hauled fresh water from a small lake for cooking and washing,

Naskusp, Arrow Lakes circa 1919, etching drypoint, 10½" x 16¾" COLLECTION OF THE ART GALLERY OF GREATER VICTORIA, REPRODUCED FROM THE UHTHOFF FAMILY COLLECTION, PHOTOGRAPHER UNKNOWN

Vancouver from the Rowing Club, circa 1914, ink on paper 4½" x 6¾", COLLECTION OF THE VANCOUVER ART GALLERY, REPRODUCED FROM JOHN UHTHOFF'S SLIDES, JOY/MICHAEL UHTHOFF COLLECTION, DIGITALLY RESTORED BY JANET DWYER

with the stark Kokanee Glacier and cedar trees in the background. Just to keep warm in the winter took much more effort than it had in Scotland. Ina recalled in her notes, first titled "Post Graduation Trip to British Columbia," that they did all their own housework, chopping wood, preserving and preparing the food, but men were hired to care for the animals. Initially stunned by the contrast to urban life in Scotland, she noted that another friend, a dentist from Edinburgh, was glorying in the escape.[4] Despite these difficulties, Ina had positive memories of the ranch (it was good fly-fishing country) and she continued her work as an artist.[5]

Work dated during this first trip suggests that Ina also journeyed to Vancouver. She created pen and ink sketches, linocuts and etchings entitled *Hastings Street, Vancouver from Kitsilano, Vancouver from the Rowing Club, Nakusp, Arrow Lakes.* These works demonstrated her skilled observation of urban scenes, but more importantly they show her desire to capture the rugged Canadian landscape that was so new to her. Ina wrote later that the land "was crying out to be recorded in pencil, paint, oils, and watercolours,"[6] a call she would respond to for decades to come.

While in Crawford Bay, Ina met her future husband, Edward (Ted) Joseph Uhthoff (1885–1971), a young, tall, independent homesteader and budding orchardist from Britain (born in Bayswater, London). They both loved the striking scenery and challenge of the Canadian west, yet shared urban upbringings with an appreciation for literature, history and art as well as training in sketching and drawing. His parents were Ludolfo (Louis) Uhthoff (born in Vera Cruz, Mexico, though the family was originally from Prussia) and Adelaida Micaela Fesser (born in Havana, Cuba).[7] Ted's mother died when he was only three. Ina's loss of her father and Ted's loss of his mother at an early age likely increased their sense of attachment.

Ludolfo Uhthoff had taken over his family's private banking and commission merchant's business (Uhthoff & Company), and when he died in 1903, Ted inherited a share of the estate. He then immigrated, landing at St. John, New Brunswick in March 1911, and made his way to Crawford Bay, where he established an apple ranch. He was remembered as having boundless energy and a mischievous sense of

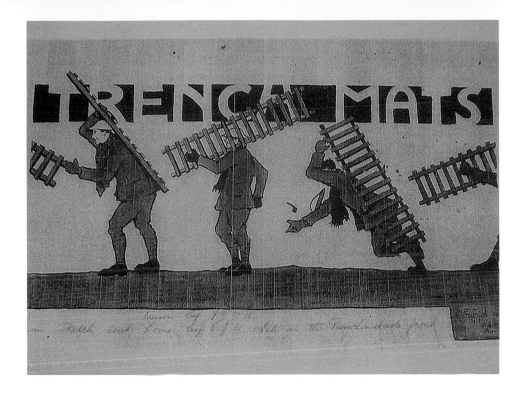

humour. Their daughter, Muriel, later felt he was so generous that he would say yes more often than not in order to be loved.[8] Ina appeared to be an attractive match for him, but World War I intervened.

Ina returned to Glasgow, while Ted joined the 54th Kootenay Batallion CEF,[9] seeing action at both Vimy Ridge and Passchendaele.[10] Entering as a private, he attained the rank of lieutenant and earned a military medal (which he never spoke about) for

> his daring coolness and devotion to duty during an attack on enemy posts on… the nights of September 5th and 6th, 1917. During that action this man observed that one of our posts was being hard pressed. He immediately crossed the road in face of heavy enemy fire and lent his assistance to the hard pressed garrison. From this post he made several individual sallies, bombing the enemy and inflicting much damage. His splendid example was an inspiration to all the men around him, and was a steadying factor at a critical time.[11]

Ted documented his participation at Passchendaele in a 1917 sketch that he sent home.[12] His interest and capability in the visual arts is evident in the drawing *Trench Mats*, depicting soldiers carrying ladders while on the front. Ina and Ted would reunite after the war.

Trench Mats, Passchenduele, 1917
pencil on paper
DRAWING BY TED UHTHOFF, UHTHOFF/
WHITE COLLECTION

THREE

Teaching and Marriage in Scotland

While Ted was serving in the war, Ina took professional training under the Glasgow Provincial Committee for the Training of Teachers. By July 1916, at 26, she was given provisional recognition (pending completion of a probation period) by the Scotch Education Department as a qualified Teacher of Drawing.[1] William Marshall, Headmaster of Provanside Higher Grade School, wrote her a glowing recommendation in July 1917:

> She is a most *competent* and *effective* teacher of her subject, and although many of her classes have been larger than usual on account of the diffi-culties of the time, she has maintained discipline and order with an ease which is somewhat rare in the case of a young teacher.[2]

Ina taught there until January 1918; Marshall later noted that she taught with "great ability and success: she is an expert in her subject and will be found a valuable member of the staff of any school, especially where advanced work

‹ *Untitled,* n.d., conté on paper, 9¾" x 13"
MICHAEL UHTHOFF COLLECTION
PHOTO BY JANET DWYER

13

Ina D.D. Uhthoff, n.d.
IMAGE #F-09355
COURTESY OF ROYAL BC
MUSEUM, BC ARCHIVES

is done."[3] Ina then taught at Onslow Drive Public School, where headmaster Jas[per] Ross recommended her, "without hesitation or difficulty,"[4] as a "teacher of great refinement and outstanding ability." Family members recalled the story that she taught at a school for "wayward boys" and that she became very good at wrapping knuckles with her ruler. Ina was known for being a strict disciplinarian who took no nonsense from the "unruly youths" who were her pupils.[5]

In her recollections, Ina wrote, "The work at the public schools was very heavy, the chief hurdle being able to preserve discipline, as a minimum sixty hefty teen-age boys composed each of the eight classes that comprised my daily programme."[6] She knew that the Headmaster of the school and the Assistant Principal could be called upon in case of emergency, but she determined that she needed to stand on her own: "So the only way in which I could tackle a job like this was to win the interest and cooperation of my classes." The strap was commonly used, but when Ina thought of "really hitting those often surly youths, I inwardly quailed." She cringed at the idea of missing the target ("a small area of bare skin on the palm of each hand"), but if she were accurate, it would establish her authority as a disciplinarian. She recalled her first use of the strap and its effect.

> Somewhat to my surprise it worked! The boys became interested in drawing and painting and from then on there was more co-operation but even now I break into a cold sweat when I think of what would probably have happened had I missed my aim![7]

At the time Ina was taking classes and teaching, Glasgow was known to be a tough city, with the reputation of High Street and the gangs called "Redskins," who appeared during the evening hours. Ina's older brother, Alec, would escort her to her night classes, calling back for her at 9:30 PM. Another frightening aspect was the "herds of cattle that made the High Street their way of access to the slaughterhouse... They were probably quite peaceful animals but anything with cloven hoofs and branching horns struck immediate terror into my heart."[8]

On the other hand, she certainly appreciated the urban sophistication, living on the Westside in the Kelvinside District near the Botanical Gardens,[9] the University of Glasgow and the Kelvingrove Museum and Art Gallery. The city was still thriving with her alma mater, the Glasgow School of Art, and the circles of culture around Charles Rennie Mackintosh, including Miss Cranston's Tea Rooms. They were furnished with stylish decorations, such as wooden panels embellished with heart and spade shapes. Teaching provided a steady salary, which as a young woman she thoroughly enjoyed: "My home life was a comfortable one so I could indulge in extravagant living!" Glasgow was "world famous [for] dress materials so I had a good time buying all I wanted with my pay cheques."[10] Ina's clothing designs included sketches of hat styles and dress designs.

While teaching, Ina stayed active as an artist, participating in group shows with both the Royal Glasgow Institute of Fine Arts and the Royal Scottish Academy in 1916.[11] In 1917, she had a solo exhibition of her Canadian scenes at the Ralph Proud Gallery in Glasgow.[12] Other works from this time reveal her love of the Scottish land-

Original designs by Ina D.D. Uhthoff, circa 1916–1926, *Street Frock of Elderberry Homespun: Accents in citron green. Bolt in citron and elephant grey suede. This design is intended for a Tall, Slim Figure as it gives width in its lines,* pencil and watercolour on paper, 12" x 9"
NANCY WHITE COLLECTION
PHOTO BY NANCY WHITE

Street Suit of Brown Tweed, hat to match, pencil on paper, 11½" x 7"
NANCY WHITE COLLECTION
PHOTO BY NANCY WHITE

Untitled (Winter with
Sled), circa 1930s, oil
REPRODUCED FROM JOHN
UHTHOFF'S SLIDES,
JOY/MICHAEL UHTHOFF
PRIVATE COLLECTION
DIGITALLY RESTORED BY JANET DWYER

› *Untitled* (Three Men at
Table), 1919, watercolour
on board, 3¾" x 5¾"
NANCY WHITE COLLECTION
PHOTO BY NANCY WHITE

scape, such as the river scene *On the Falloch, Perthshire*, and the untitled watercolour
of winter trees on page 6, one of the few works signed with her maiden name. Ina's
files also include an undated certificate stating that she was elected to the Royal
Society for the Encouragement of Arts, Manufacturers and Commerce, London.[13]

During these years, Ina corresponded with Ted, who had left the armed forces
when World War I ended, one of many wounded soldiers. The stark black-and-white
painting of three men at a table, dated 1919 though signed Ina D.D. Uhthoff, is from
this period.[14] In a photograph from February of that year, Ina leans against rocks,
walking stick in hand, at Buxton, Derbyshire, England.[15] Did Ted Uhthoff take this
while on a hike with her? There is no inscription, but in 1919, she stopped teaching at
Onslow Drive Public School, and they married in June. The war was over; they had
survived, and Ted and Ina looked forward to happier times.

On the Falloch, Perthshire, n.d., watercolour on paper, 6½" x 9½"
MICHAEL UHTHOFF COLLECTION, PHOTO BY JANET DWYER

Ina as hiker, Buxton, Derbyshire, circa 1919
UHTHOFF/WHITE COLLECTION

FOUR

Kootenays to the Capital: The Victoria School of Art Years

AFTER MARRIAGE IN SCOTLAND, Ted and Ina Uhthoff sailed from Liverpool to Canada in May, returning to the stunning beauty of the Kootenays where they had first met. They then spent two months in Vancouver, going back in September to their home in Crawford Bay, where Ted could continue to pursue his interest in being an orchardist. Ina later wrote.

> The house was small but had charm and stood in magnificent surroundings. The life there was a strenuous one consisting of early rising and long hours of physical labour, but there were many compensations. We grew our own food. I made my own butter and bread. We cured our own hams, preserved our own fruits and vegetables, caught fish in the near-by creek and lake, shot grouse in the season and canned them.[1]

Activities at the community hall included an exhibition of artistic talent (though Ina is not mentioned), the Crawford Bay Dramatic and Musical Society

‹ *Untitled* (Trees by the River), n.d., watercolour on paper, 20" x 15"
NANCY WHITE
COLLECTION
PHOTO BY NANCY WHITE

(where Ted's songs and recitation with a friend scored a "distinct hit"), Women's Institute meetings and sports days, and the December Turkey Shoots and Children's Christmas Tree Party.[2] Crawford Bay (and neighboring Gray Creek) thrived economically, shipping (in 1920) 816 boxes of fall apples.

⌒ Ted Uhthoff, circa 1919

⌒⟩ Ina (Campbell) Uhthoff, circa 1919
PHOTOS COURTESY OF JOY UHTHOFF

⟩⌒ Ted Uhthoff with daughter Muriel, Crawford Bay cabin, BC

⟩⟩⌒ Ina with son John, circa 1923, Crawford Bay cabin, BC
PHOTOS COURTESY OF NANCY WHITE

On August 3, 1920, their first child, John Campbell Uhthoff, was born.[3] Despite the peaceful lush landscape, so enticing for a painter and fruit farmer, Ina was challenged to cope with an infant and maintain the hard-working pace of being a pioneer's wife. She likely became homesick and felt isolated in the remote community and longed for the comfort and support of her sister and mother in Glasgow. By April 1922, Ina was again pregnant and in May made arrangements to visit her mother and sister Lily in Glasgow, departing with son John in July on the ss *Montrose* from Montreal for Liverpool. Ina and Ted's second child, Muriel Irene Campbell Uhthoff, was born on December 9, 1922, in Scotland.

When Muriel was less than a year old, Ina and the two children returned to Crawford Bay.[4] A diary, probably written by Ted, noted in red letters that "Ina, John, and Baby leave for Canada" on April 19, 1923. By May, the family was reunited. Subsequent diary entries documented Muriel's christening on July 21, cutting her first teeth throughout the summer, her ability to stand up holding onto things by October 1 and her first birthday.[5] Photos show the simple wooden cabin with a front garden, Muriel in a Borden's Evaporated Milk box and John in a sunhat seated

behind his laughing baby sister. Though Ina must have had little time for art, her linocut of Kootenay Mountain is dated from this period.

Ina may have longed to establish herself as a teacher and artist in a stimulating urban setting but she also needed to become the breadwinner, as one reporter wrote a few years later in the *Daily Colonist*, "Mrs Uhthoff resumed her career after her marriage owing to the fact that her husband was incapacitated by wounds received in the Great War." So in 1923, not long after returning from Scotland with her children, she began to make her first forays to live and work in Victoria.[6] By 1924, she had collected references[7] and taught at the Summer School for Teachers in Victoria,[8] clearly paving her way to move. The children remained in Crawford Bay until she could establish herself, and

John and sister Muriel, summer 1923, Crawford Bay, BC, PHOTO COURTESY OF NANCY WHITE

Ina and baby Muriel, 1923, Crawford Bay cabin, BC
PHOTO COURTESY OF IOY UHTHOFF

Kootenay Mountain
1923–24, linocut on
paper, 8½" x 11"
NANCY WHITE
COLLECTION

there is only conjecture about why they stayed with friends (not with their father).[9] No Uhthoffs are listed in Crawford Bay between 1923 and 1925. Probably Ted's "war wounds" made it difficult for him to cope. Many soldiers suffered serious and long-lasting psychological damage due to shell shock and post-traumatic stress disorder, including emotional numbing, recurring nightmares and feeling disconnected from family and friends. (During World War I, British forces lost 80,000 soldiers, one-seventh of all disability discharges, to shell shock.) John, then five years old, later described his view of that time as "a long dark tunnel with no light at the end."[10] The adventure of living as a family in the Kootenays had come to an end.

Ina finally relocated to the capital city and, by the fall of 1925,[11] established herself as a busy and hardworking young teacher, artist and community member. Determination and flexibility were the key traits that steered her through the subsequent decades as a responsible mother and a dedicated educator. Though the Island Arts and Crafts Club had started a School of Handicraft and Design in 1913, it was short-lived. The Provincial Arts and Industrial Institute had merged with the club in 1922, forming the Island Arts and Crafts Society (IACS). Classes were available with individual artists, notably Margaret Kitto, a stalwart of the group who taught in her studio, rented rooms in the Union Bank Building. It was also a good time to set up teaching practical arts, because in 1925 Dr. J. Harold Putnam (Inspector of Schools, Ottawa) and Dr. George M. Weir (Professor of Education at the University of British Columbia) produced the Putnam Weir Survey that strongly endorsed "progressivism" and recommended enriching the Canadian curriculum with a number of subjects, including manual arts.[12] Ina recalled that, when she first came to British Columbia, "flat copy" (copying from another drawing, not using a model to see three dimensions) was the approach to drawing and painting in the private schools, but not in the classes under government control.[13] William P. Weston,[14] the well-known educator and artist, impressed her with his work in the Vancouver schools and his book on high-school art, which Ina would have used when teaching. Like Weston, she spent increasing time painting landscapes.

Ina also remembered Charles H. Scott (a Scot from the GSA), a hard worker and competent draftsman, who was key to launching the Vancouver School of Decorative and Applied Arts, first as Principal and then Director in 1925.[15] The aim was to "steer a course in Art that would enable students to land either on the shores of industry or the less secure footing of the fine arts."[16] Although meetings between Charles and Ina were not documented, it is intriguing that two former GSA students would head art schools in the two major cities of British Columbia at this time.

Ina made quite a splash when she exhibited for the first time at the IACS's 16th Annual Exhibition of Paintings, Drawings, Designs and Crafts in October 1925. The exhibition at the Crystal Gardens was an excellent venue to display her capabilities to people who might want to take art classes, purchase her work or hire her for portraiture. She included landscapes in watercolour, oil, pastels and etchings, showing scenes from Glasgow as well as from B.C., such as Nakusp and Beacon Hill Park. Ina entered a variety of portraits, and the one of Mrs. A.M.D. Fairbairn, wife of the Private Secretary to the Lieutenant-Governor, must have gained credibility for her in the city. The *Victoria Daily Colonist* newspaper gave her positive coverage:

> There is an unusually big list of new exhibitors, particularly in water colors, oils, and pastels sections as several of the newcomers are really distinguished artists. Their entries add greatly to the exhibition as a whole. Among the new exhibitors is Mrs. Ina D.D. Uhthoff, who came to Victoria from the Old Land

about a year ago, just too late to enter anything in the 1924 exhibition. Mrs. Uhthoff has water colors, oils, pastels, and etchings in the collections, showing conspicuously fine work in each section.[17]

Ina also submitted pieces to the Crafts section–copper and enamel work, such as the triptych with St. Catherine. At this exhibit were the artists who Ina would interact, work, volunteer and exhibit with for many years. In addition to Emily Carr and A.M.D. Fairbairn, there were amateur artists including Josephine Crease (later the Honorary President of the IACS), Maude Lettice and Martha Harris. Another consistent exhibitor well into the 1950s was Will Menelaws, a fellow Scot educated at the Royal Scottish Academy in Edinburgh, who taught art at Oak Bay Secondary and Glenlyon Schools.[18]

By 1926, Ina opened and was listed as Principal of the Victoria School of Art at 410–620 View Street. This location had been the site of the Western Art Studio, run by artist Margaret Kitto until her death in 1925, the year that Ina started teaching

Home of the Victoria School of Art, 1926, 620 View Street, Victoria, BC
PHOTO BY AUTHOR, 2011

there.[19] It was close to the rooms of the IACS, whose members could be of support. The school offered a wide range of courses, reflecting the scope of arts in the IACS exhibitions. Classes included drawing and painting, figure drawing, portraiture, book illustration, design and commercial art, posters and lettering, etching, black and white, as well as outdoor sketching. A special class on Saturday mornings for children, at a reduced fee, prepared them for drawing examinations.[20] The curriculum showed Ina's versatility and enterprise, as well as her awareness of what students needed to seriously further their education. She probably used her own earlier work as examples for her students, which might explain why some are dated before her marriage but signed with her married name, Uhthoff, instead of Campbell. Also, Ina may have wanted the consistency of one name when she exhibited her work in order to build her reputation. It was not long before her students who had completed two years were readily accepted at the Vancouver schools of art for further instruction.[21] She knew how to train and promote her pupils. In class, she was always formally addressed as "Mrs. Uhthoff."

In 1926, Ted is again listed as a rancher in Crawford Bay, and Ina is Principal of the Victoria School of Art. By then, the children were in Victoria; Muriel turning four and John entering grade one. Though the children were probably happy to be with their mother in a neighborhood of many families, Ina had to be frugal in her finances and enterprising in her social connections. John recalled that she spent a great deal of the day away from her children: "She was always going away in the morning and coming back in the evening. Ultimately, she hired a woman, an old Scot," who looked after them for years.[22]

Their home at 591 St. Patrick Street in south Oak Bay was conveniently near Monterey Elementary School, which her children attended. During the next year, Ted was listed as living with them on nearby St. David Street and worked for the Royal Financial Corporation, but by 1928, he is not listed in directories as living with them, though they visited each other.

The first exhibit of Ina's art students occurred from mid-April to May 1, 1926, in the Union Bank Building studio. The newspaper account is glowing, stating that it is "one of the most interesting art students' exhibitions assembled in the city... a group of serious workers, many of whom show evidence of gifts of unique character." The art included crayons and pastel drawings, pen-and-ink work and oil paintings. The mark of the Uhthoff studio present in the students' work showed "breadth of style, a freedom and grace of technique, sound draughtsmanship, orderliness, proportion, and sense of values, and, in fact, a combination of qualities which make for distinction." The critic felt that the least observant would be able to spot the model a hundred miles from Victoria after seeing the old gentlemen's likeness in the works shown.[23] The exhibit opened daily at midday and closed at 10 PM, accommodating almost anyone's schedule.

In May 1927, another student exhibition opened at the Yates Street Arcade, showing Ina to be an eclectic and highly regarded teacher. A reviewer noted that the "work was far above the general standard of art students' displays."[24] One group studied

Victoria School of Art advertisement, St. Margaret's School Magazine, June 1926, page 7, COURTESY OF ST. MARGARET'S SCHOOL ARCHIVES

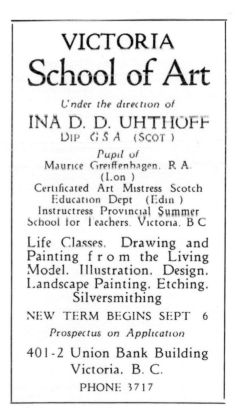

VICTORIA
School of Art

Under the direction of

INA D. D. UHTHOFF
DIP G S A (SCOT)

Pupil of
Maurice Greiffenhagen, R.A.
(Lon.)
Certificated Art Mistress Scotch
Education Dept. (Edin.)
Instructress Provincial Summer
School for Teachers, Victoria, B C

Life Classes, Drawing and Painting from the Living Model, Illustration, Design, Landscape Painting, Etching, Silversmithing

NEW TERM BEGINS SEPT 6

Prospectus on Application

401-2 Union Bank Building
Victoria, B. C.
PHONE 3717

Celtic art; another group went "exhaustively" into Egyptian, Grecian and Phoenician galleys, and a third group viewed dress through the ages in poster making and book illustrations. The reviewer commented, "Mrs. Uhthoff obviously does not try to impose her own style on her students, but rather seeks to develop the individual talent and expression of each pupil" so that, though the subjects may be identical, there was infinite variety expressed in the art.[25] The youngest tots as well as some older students worked from models of animals—no copying from other drawings was allowed. What variety! Bunnies, parrots, roosters, guinea pigs, pigeons and pet canaries were all subjects for the students' developing art. With children of her own, Ina had a deep understanding of what young people could create and effective strategies for shepherding their talents. Her own son John's sketches exemplify the artistic skills that she surely fostered.

The reviewer described the life-class work in detail, explaining the many steps, usually starting with the head. There would be "snapshot" drawings, which were then anatomized to show the bony framework. Eventually, the students would work up to a complete outline, using a living model, showing the lines of body and limbs in action, followed by the techniques of blocking in, massing of light and shade, the study of bony detail and the principal muscles of the face and neck. For portraits, students spent time learning about the constructive lines of the head in different positions, for example, front and three-quarter views, as well as several classes on the detail of eyes, nose, ear and mouth. Casts were used for the study of hands and feet. The oils created by older students revealed the value of this time and effort spent in preparatory work.

Travel posters for India and Burma included Phoebe Fuller's "blazing, gorgeously opulent poster of mahout-driven elephants under swaying colored parasols."[26] Students also designed posters for a masquerade ball, for the slogan "Follow the Birds to Victoria" and for the theme "Victoria the Garden City." Additional works comprised designs for fans, fruit labels, book covers and illustrations. Another student of note, Olive Acton, showed a range of work—a striking wallpaper design employing Celtic motifs, a floral motif applied to a black Spanish shawl and a black evening frock of Vogue design. One of Olive's designs, which employed a First Nation theme, was chosen for the casket presented to Governor General Lord Willingdon, who had recently received "freedom of the city"; student Beth Grimison used the same theme for the scroll enclosed in the casket.[27]

By the summer of 1927, the Victoria School of Art, in need of larger quarters, moved to 1385 Manor Road. Due to recent redecoration, the rooms were spacious, light, airy and attractive. There was ample space for the different departments, and the balconies were considered "splendid vantage points for landscape sketching." The expanded curriculum offered an array of choices in many media,[28] supporting the recognition of fine and applied arts in exhibitions.[29] Ina employed a wide variety of models for her classes, demonstrated by her own accomplishments in portraiture. Those unable to attend could take a correspondence course.[30] To entice potential students, Ina further suggested that a long and expensive journey to the east or "Old Country" centres was unnecessary, since an efficient, quality school was right in Victoria.[31]

Like now famous painter Emily Carr, who resorted in tradition-bound Victoria to hooking rugs and making pottery with First Nations designs for the tourist trade, an artist in this small capital city needed to be versatile to make ends meet. The IACS exhibits included hooked rugs, weavings, needlework, pottery, china painting, leatherwork, metal work and woodwork (and even art made from fish scales and shells).[32] First Nation designs were popular, and art collected on trips abroad or through the family would also be exhibited. In 1928, the Victoria Technical School showed copper repoussé, hand-wrought iron and lathe work, as well as a Davenport table.[33] The Women's Institute contributed a B.C. wool exhibit and related textile creations. Though painting and drawing were strongly represented over the years, there was comparatively little sculpture. Ina's school embraced this stance of fostering a variety of arts, many with commercial and practical applications.

To further establish herself in Victoria, Ina did more than initiate her own art school. Starting with eye-catching entries in 1925, she participated through the late 1940s in IACS's exhibitions until the group transformed into the Victoria Sketch Club, which is still active.[34] Though she usually showed the "fine" art of painting and drawing, she also contributed to the crafts section: in 1928, a *Stained Wood and Gesso Panel*

Jamaican, circa early 1930s, oil on canvas
19½" x 16"
MICHAEL UHTHOFF
COLLECTION
PHOTO BY JANET DWYER

Girl with Red Kerchief
n.d., oil on canvas
13" x 11", NANCY WHITE
COLLECTION

PHOTO BY NANCY WHITE

and a *Felt Decorated Bag*. With her Haida rug design she joined the popular trend of appropriating First Nations art. In the same show, Emily Carr exhibited a hooked rug with First Nation motifs. Like Emily, Ina was ingenious in making a living in the arts, and these shows linked her with well-to-do families, those most likely to buy her work and enroll themselves and their children in her classes. She also aligned herself with the Church of England (Anglican Church),[35] another tie to the right community. Ina was not remembered as heavily involved with church work or politics, but "loyalty to the King" was important.[36]

Ina also was associated with St. Margaret's School for girls. In 1928, the School Prospectus listed Mrs. I. Uhthoff as Staff for Art.[37] Another staff member, Mrs. Minna Gildea, opened the Strathcona Lodge School (Shawnigan Lake) in 1927, where, according to John, his mother taught for a while.[38] When Ina began there is unclear, but she definitely taught in the mid-to-late 1930s, probably in exchange for tuition fees[39] when her daughter, Muriel, was a student.

In 1927, Ina Uhthoff again taught at the Provincial Summer School for Teachers. She recalled that the programme was valuable, in that teachers from across Canada could get credits for teaching certificates with the seal of the Department of Education. With the large classes and the high standard of work,[40] the teaching was strenuous for her. However, it was not all work; she remembered "happy days" in the early gatherings at Victoria High School. Famous musicians gave concerts and dances, picnics and excursions drew the students together to form lasting friendships.[41] Ina continued this teaching through 1934.[42]

A key person for the Summer School was educator John Kyle. John Uhthoff remembered him as a "happy, roly-poly florid face Scot" who was friendly and a good friend of his mother.[43] Kyle had been instrumental in providing art education in Vancouver before being appointed Organizer of Technical Education for the province in 1914.[44] Like Charles H. Scott and Grace Melvin, he had come from Britain and, with them, was instrumental in developing art education in the Provincial Summer

School (to upgrade teachers) started in 1914, probably initiated by Kyle; Ina noted that he was responsible for much of the development of the crafts in the 1923 session.[45] She was grateful to him because he supplied the means for her to carry out plans for her school: "He held the purse strings that provided me with the material to work with."[46]

When the Victoria School of Art moved to Manor Road near Craigdarroch Castle (then Victoria College), Ina offered correspondence courses, an option that Kyle may have influenced. He was probably the valuable link for her becoming an art instructor for the Secondary School Correspondence Course, a government job that gave her a steady and dependable income for thirty years.[47] Ina continued with her residence and school on Manor Road in 1928.

Ina's many pen-and-ink sketches of life in early British Columbia illustrated the Women's Canadian Club's 1928 publication, *The Pioneer Women of Vancouver Island 1843–1866*.[48] Scenes included standard views of Fort Victoria, Craigflower School, Captain William Henry McNeill's trading boat *The Beaver*, a warship in Esquimalt Harbour, a water cart, and a nun from the Sisters of St. Ann.[49]

The club launched the book at a "Pioneer Tea" at the Empress Hotel in November 1928. A feature of the stage decorations was a massive single-panel screen in the form of a poster illustrating Ina Uhthoff's front cover design. Ina sat at the head table with the Lieutenant Governor, the club's president and past president, as well as the many members of the Book Committee, comprising most of the elite of Victoria, including Annie Bullen who was in charge of artistic features.[50] Annie and other members of the Island Arts and Crafts Society (IACS) (such as Josephine Crease and Martha Harris, daughter of Sir James Douglas), who were also seated at the head table, were the target of Emily Carr's vehemence about staid Victoria art tastes. Carr, a native daughter of Victoria, could have easily done the sketches for the book, but she wasn't interested in social obligations although she did accommodate them with an occasional talk. In 1927, she had finally gained some national recognition; her paintings of First Nations people and places had been included in the National Gallery of Canada's (NGC) Exhibition of Canadian West Coast Art. By 1928, Carr had sold work to buyers such as the NGC and embarked on another trip to First Nations villages in northern B.C. Furthermore, Carr's irascible and unpredictable behaviour was probably no match for the astute diplomacy, manners and propriety of Ina Uhthoff in

dealing with stalwarts of the Women's Canadian Club. Also Ina had the urgent need to support herself and her children, so she was in no position to ruffle feathers.

The author, Nancy de Bertrand Lugrin, and the Provincial Archivist, John Hosie, spoke. He pointed out that, for many years, "it had been the custom, when speaking about pioneers, to think of them in terms of man and not of the woman; but the man would have been of very little use without the valiant support of his wife"; thus he was glad that the Women's Canadian Club had memorialized the women pioneers at last.[51] Ina was introduced, and gave special tribute to the club members and women from the Provincial Library for their assistance. No doubt they were able to obtain sketches and photographs that would have aided Ina in depicting the early scenes on Vancouver Island. The celebration included, of course, the pouring of tea, as well as the Empress orchestra and vocalists accompanied by a pianist.

While at ease with the traditional elite of Victoria's art circles, Ina also respected the work of maverick artist Emily Carr. Both were inspired by B.C.'s natural scenery and consistently experimented in their painting to explore new aesthetic expressions. When Carr had participated in the Exhibition of Canadian West Coast Art, she had traveled east for the opening and met artists Lawren Harris and other members of the Group of Seven. Inspired by them, she sketched during the summer of 1928 in northern B.C. and the Queen Charlotte Islands. That September, Ina joined Carr in sponsoring a master class at her own studio and Emily's studio with Seattle artist Mark Tobey.[52] Known now as an abstract expressionist, who was "a mystical painter" and sometimes Cubist in his work, he founded the Northwest School, an art movement based in Skagit County, Washington.[53] For his time, he was an individualistic and innovative artist whose teaching technique was a "sort of receptive method." Older students were told to "start with the imagination," then "go out and look at things, to study them, and that will stimulate your retentive memory and your retentive memory will bring it back to your imagination again."[54] Five or six painters worked with Tobey, including George Napier, who was reported to have had considerable ability, even though he was a "Sunday painter." He was apparently distressed at Emily's poverty and helped her financially by taking lessons and buying her paintings.[55] Ina reminisced that her work with Tobey had inspired her,[56] and she experimented more with non-objective art. He also taught at her studio in 1929 and 1930.[57] Though she gained a new vision through Tobey, Ina never felt that she had adequate time to develop it because she was so busy working to survive during the Depression. Nonetheless, this boost to her art probably led to her exhibiting for the first time with the B.C. Society of Artists in May 1929.[58] The next year, Ina was one of the B.C. artists selected for the Canadian National Exhibition in Vancouver, showing *Turret Mountain*, *Paddy* and *Portrait Study*.[59] Two other Victoria artists were represented: Emily Carr and Will Menelaws. Another "Unheralded Artist of B.C.," Mildred Valley Thornton, exhibited, but at that time she was listed as being from Saskatchewan.[60]

In August 1929, Ina and the children joined Ted in Sardis, B.C., and later for Christmas; after the holiday, she and the children were bound for Victoria in her Essex car.[61] Though Ina and her children moved more than ten times between 1926 and 1944 they usually lived in south Oak Bay, close to schools.[62] One of John's friends (Peter Hinton), who grew up on Beach Drive, remembered Ina as being "motherly."[63] Muriel's longtime friend, Sue Horton, recalled that when she went for supper, the meal might not be ready and Ina would be painting at the kitchen table. It was a frugal household with little entertaining and few parties in the home.[64] Thisbe Fletcher (later Stewart), another friend, vividly remembered Ina's generosity in transport-

Untitled (Pioneer Woman and Baby on Horse), 1928 etching, COURTESY OF THE WOMEN'S CANADIAN CLUB OF CANADA, PHOTO BY CHRISTINA JOHNSON-DEAN

Craigflower School 1928, etching COURTESY OF THE WOMEN'S CANADIAN CLUB OF CANADA PHOTO BY AUTHOR

ing the family in her car with the "cellophane flaps" to the tennis courts, started by her father Percy Fletcher in Oak Bay. Muriel loved tennis and won awards; Ina later taught with Fletcher at Glenlyon School. Both Thisbe and her mother, Florence (Florrie), took art lessons from Ina; Thisbe recalled that, though her mother was an amateur watercolourist, she wanted to do more than paint "pretty little pictures." Students could be intimidated by Ina and be shy of criticisms. Thisbe remembered that Ina would utter "ummm" when she approved. She would never correct a student's drawing, but she might put a small "x" on a spot and suggest a change: "She would not do it for you." Ina was the "only working mother" that Thisbe knew, and she felt a special kinship to her, just as she believed Muriel felt towards Florrie. When the girls visited the downtown library, Muriel would borrow cookbooks, instead of novels. She loved to cook and set the table, making it easier on her mother. One favourite recipe was for Scottish shortbread.[65] Like many families, they rode bikes throughout the community. Muriel recalled that her mother bought a player piano, and they would listen to music while watching the keys move. They had happy times in summer, visiting Sooke where they had long walks to the candy store and learned about "dirt gardening," presumably being hands-on in the garden. She thought of Vancouver as a "brassy Canadian town moneywise and full of prairie people," whereas Victoria was perhaps more British, but "pretentious." "More than anything," Muriel wrote, "we wanted a home that was lovely and warm and secure."[66] Ina kept in touch with her sisters, Edie and Lily, who had moved to Santa Barbara, California. Due to distance, there was less contact with her sister Kate, who had gone to Vienna to be a governess, and her brother Alec, who had married a woman named Meg, and continued to live in Glasgow. Ina's three sisters never married, and none of her siblings had children.

For years after the 1929 economic crash, taking art lessons was not seen as essential for many families. Ina was known for being exceedingly thrifty.[67] By 1929, the Victoria School of Art was at 739 Yates Street; the next year, 612 View Street. Despite the lean times, in the summer of 1931, Ina did take the children by ship to San Diego,

Dandelions in the Wind
n.d., oil, 13½" x 15¼"
MICHAEL UHTHOFF
COLLECTION
PHOTO BY JANET DWYER

INA D. D. UHTHOFF

California, to visit her sisters in Santa Barbara.[68] Ina's drawings of ships may date from these trips. By age 11, John was developing the artistic talents of his mother, and he carefully drew the ss *Emma Alexander*. Upon their return, he spent the winter of 1931–1932 with his father, who again lived in Crawford Bay and worked at the W.O. Burden camp (probably logging). Compared to Victoria, life in the backwoods was more challenging; the only light came from Coleman lamps. When school was out, Ina and Muriel came to spend the summer with them. Other summer visits followed for John, including 1934 when he and his father camped at X-Ray Lake and climbed to the summit of Old Tom Mountain.[69]

In 1931, Ina Uhthoff was included in *Who's Who in British Columbia*.[70] While operating her Victoria School of Art, she also started teaching art in 1933 at Glenlyon School (for boys) in her neighborhood at 1377 St. David Street (before moving to its current location, architect Francis Rattenbury's home, on Beach Drive). She also instituted the Art Display at the annual Prize Giving and continued until 1938, when she handed her responsibilities to a fellow Scot, Will Menelaws, whom she considered an artist of integrity.[71] Along with the conservative members of the IACS, Ina knew younger artists such as Max Maynard, Jack Shadbolt and Edythe Hembroff. In Canada the Group of Seven dominated the new national art scene, and internationally, surrealism, abstract expressionism and indigenous arts were gaining broader attention.

In 1932, Max Maynard, an elementary school teacher, was Vice President of the IACS and convinced them to allow a Modern Room at the annual exhibition. Ina "badly wanted to be represented"[72] in this section, but Maynard, the organizer, allowed her to show only one of her paintings, *Cedars*, probably a simple flowing charcoal sketch of the iconic tree.[73] All her other works were in the conservative rooms: four pleasant watercolours from her trip to Santa Barbara and an oil of Kokanee Glacier.[74] Ina also participated in the crafts section, which listed names of exhibitors but not directly with any creation; included were rugs, embroidery, tooled leather, flowers, lampshades, parchment work, hand-painted cards and calendars, as well as "numerous novelties."[75] Her colleague Edythe Hembroff commented later that Ina's entry "testified to her sure sense of line and composition." Edythe had originally noted that Ina's work had not changed notably after the Modern Room. Though she found Ina to be an accomplished painter, always striving for new insights, she remarked that "it was not until the early forties that she caught with

Mountain Shadows, n.d.
watercolour, 12½" x 9¼"
IMAGE #M964.1.64
COURTESY OF UNIVERSITY OF
VICTORIA ART COLLECTIONS,
COLLECTION OF JOHN AND
KATHERINE MALTWOOD
UNIVERSITY OF VICTORIA ART
COLLECTIONS PHOTO

John and Muriel, 1929,
on the S.S. *Emma
Alexander* to San Diego
PHOTO COURTESY OF
NANCY WHITE

even a pale imitation of Cubism."[76] According to art historian Maria Tippett, "unlike Maynard and Shadbolt... Uhthoff did not dissect and intellectually analyze the elements of nature, but sought expression of the surface reality of landscape, capturing the lyricism of nature's patterns."[77] Ina could play many angles; she was not caught in any manifesto, certainly not one that might offend the conservative people who supported her school.

Max Maynard was the self-elected juror for the Modern Room and built this mini-show around Emily Carr, who would have insisted on including her sketching partner Edythe Hembroff. He included one of his students, 14-year-old Robert Bladen, and his friend John McDonald, who did not consider himself an artist but who had done a woodcut based on a drawing by Max. In addition, he invited Jack Shadbolt, another elementary school art teacher, though like Max, he had no formal art training. This was Jack's first show. Jack and Max sketched together and discussed poetry, literature and art, especially the ideas of the Group of Seven, described in Fred Housser's "A Canadian Art Movement."[78] Max wrote a document about his philosophy (dubbed "Max's Manifesto" by Edythe Hembroff), and he hoped to enlighten "the old fogeys" of the IACS. Unfortunately, Max left it in the room unattended one day, and no copy has survived.[79] Edythe remembered that it was based on the formulist ideas of English art critic Clive Bell, who wrote, "Art was not a matter of imitating and reproducing nature, however skillfully, but of creating the patterns, structures, and forms that underlie the confusion of natural appearance."[80] Though Ina was interested and capable of creating works that were not mere "imitations," she also knew that the buying public in Victoria would more likely appreciate and purchase representational art. All other Modern Room exhibitors (except Emily Carr who was older and passed away in 1945) moved away from the city. Only Ina continued to make a living as a professional with her art skills in conservative Victoria.

Ina's daughter recalled visiting Emily Carr during that time, probably for tea; she and her mother drove to her home in James Bay. The young Muriel did not forget the animals, especially the "parrot which made an impression" as well as large paintings that were on brown paper, one showing "above the trees." They did not see Emily Carr often, but Muriel thought the two artists admired each other. She felt that her mother's admiration for Carr was enormous and that her work was infectious.[81] In her book *Hundreds and Thousands: The Journals of An Artist*, Carr is believed to have anonymously described an encounter with Ina.

A woman came to my studio. She is an artist with two children and an invalid husband to support. I esteemed her very much. She said, "I cannot paint. It takes all my strength to support my children and bring them up to think of beautiful things, to be with them and share with them in their impressionable years. I feel if I try to teach a good *honest* commercial art that is of service to my pupils, I am doing more good than dabbling around in paint myself, doing weary and unconsciously weak work." She was really interested in my work. She said it appealed to her like religion.[82]

John recollected that his mother never seemed to have enough time to just paint.[83]

One student of this period was Audrey St. Denys (later Johnson), who became the art critic for the *Victoria Daily Times*. She wrote about showing Ina some sketches and wondered if they revealed enough talent to enrol in an art school. Ina told her that she had just closed the art school and suggested that Audrey register in the Summer School for Teachers. She followed that advice and "found it an exhilarating experience," leading to full-time studies with Ina in the fall.[84] Audrey attended life classes, learned pastel and charcoal techniques and became involved in the design-ing, carving and printing of wood and lino blocks. By 1933, she exhibited with the IACS. Audrey remembered Ina as "a skilled artist and a dedicated teacher."[85] "The most vital and exhilarating activity was taking place at this time in the studio of Ina Uhthoff, where she taught and inspired a large number of students in numer-ous techniques and all media." Audrey "relished every moment of this experience."[86] Student and teacher kept in contact, their paths crossing again when the Art Gallery of Greater Victoria was established and both wrote art reviews for local newspapers.

In 1934, Ina's work appeared in the Vancouver Art Gallery's 3rd Annual B.C. Artists exhibit (*Alpine Meadows, Windswept Tree*) and the IACS's annual show. Other Victoria artists at the former included Josephine Crease, Maude Lettice, L.A. Loveland and Gwladys Woodward. From Vancouver there was Charles Scott, Beatrice Lennie, Irene Hoffar Reid and Fred Varley. Ina continued to exhibit with the IACS; the news-paper described her contribution to the 1935 show: "Ina D.D. Uhthoff, among other examples of her work, has an arresting conventionalized study of roofs over which one sees the distant harbor."[87] However, her efforts shifted towards the larger, more cosmopolitan art scene in Vancouver. In 1936, Ina became a Fellow of the Royal Society of Arts (FRCA).[88] Muriel later wrote that her mother must have been pleased

Ina D.D. Uhthoff, 1931, in *Who's Who in British Columbia*, Victoria Carter, S.M., ed.
PHOTO COURTESY OF GREATER VICTORIA PUBLIC LIBRARY

to be able to add the RSA (Royal Scottish Academy) to her credentials, not just the GSA (Glasgow School of Art): "She could do anything she wanted with pencil, charcoal, paint and paintbrush." She noted that one reason her mother struggled to be recognized was that she was neither Canadian, American nor European; she was "from beginning to end a Scottish woman."[89]

Later that year Ina attended a theatre party and buffet supper put on by the Graduates Association for the 1936 graduating class of the Vancouver School of Decorative and Applied Arts.[90] The invitation may have been due to her many students who went to Vancouver after completing their early excellent training in her school. Though based securely in Victoria, Ina was clearly connected to the larger art community of B.C.'s bigger, more enterprising city, as well as her native Scotland.

By 1936–1937, the Victoria School of Art and Ina's residence were at 1336 Beach Drive. A poster ad for the school in 1936 detailed the staff (Principal Ina Uhthoff), the usual wide-range of courses, many flexible schedules and accommodating fees. The building was probably the "haunted house" which John referred to later;[91] Muriel also mentioned her mother's belief in ghosts, which Ina thought inhabited some of her Victoria homes.[92] John returned from living with his father in the Kootenays, and in 1935 (at 15) received the Award of Merit and Silver Medallion for completion of the Royal Life Saving Society course.[93] In grade 10, he demonstrated the positive influence of his mother's artistic capabilities by receiving an art award at Oak Bay Secondary's closing ceremonies. The family papers include a greeting card and cartoon caricatures that he drew of various people.[94] Meanwhile, Muriel remained an avid tennis player, as well as an accomplished dancer with Dorothy Cox's Western School of Dance.[95] After elementary school, Muriel attended Strathcona Lodge School in Shawnigan Lake, where Minna Gildea, Ina's colleague at St. Margaret's School, was headmistress. Muriel completed junior matriculation and won the cup for tennis. Both of Ina's children proved to be capable academically as well as in the arts and athletics, a testament to her effectiveness as a parent.

Ina often painted her Oak Bay neighbourhood, in watercolours or oils, showing the bay and boathouse, the shore with blooming flowers and Mt. Baker as seen from Cattle Point (p. vii).[96] Art must have been an island of calm in her very busy life.

In 1938, Ina was asked by the provincial government to take over the Kingston School of Pottery.[97] The location, 326 Kingston Street in James Bay, an older neighbourhood near the Parliament Buildings, was originally an elementary school. Soon it offered drawing and painting courses, which had to be regulated by the Vancouver School of Art in order to grant credits.[98]

As Ina blended her Victoria School of Art with the Kingston School of Pottery, her income became more stable, and she once again separated her home from her workplace. The family moved into 1037 Craigdarroch Road (Craigmyle House) for two years, and

Untitled (Pine Cones)
n.d., ink and watercolour
8" x 6", MICHAEL UHTHOFF
COLLECTION
PHOTO BY JANET DWYER

then to the second-floor apartment at 468 Beach Drive in Oak Bay,[99] from where she painted watercolour scenes of the straits and the Olympic Mountains. As usual, she worked extraordinarily hard for long hours to make the school viable. In addition to being the main teacher, she did administrative and janitorial work—arriving by 7 AM to stoke the furnace so that the temperature was bearable for students upon arrival.[100] John remembered working with his mother. He loved the job of mold making (for casting clay)—to him, it was fascinating.[101]

The school was already well-equipped with wheels, benches, tables and kiln for teaching pottery. John Kyle, Director of Technical Education, had instigated the kiln's installation.[102] Ina noted that, in previous years, the school "had been something of a playground for elderly ladies who wanted to earn some extra money from the sale of pottery. There was no supervision and though some of the results found a reasonably easy market, the standard of work was not high."[103] A foreman from a pottery in England was brought in to establish a more "workman-like approach to the preparation of the clay, chiefly for work on the wheel," but Ina found him wanting because he did not have "even a rudimentary idea of producing anything of aesthetic value." When Ina first came to the school, the glazes were of the "brown betty" sort, which were not very successful. Ina accepted the challenge of improving the pottery, "hardly knowing what I was letting myself in for." The trained foreman's ideas were oriented to commercial use, not artistic, and as Ina pushed for more interesting glazes, he frowned upon her attempts. She "vehemently" told him that she was not a potter, but she was an admirer of good form and colour in the craft. The education department made the offer to cover the cost of all materials, and so there was more experimentation in colourful glazes. Ina "found the research into the components of glazes of infinite interest and long hours of... work were enjoyed instead of dreaded." She also tackled the issue of basic design in order to

Untitled (Waves on Beach), n.d. watercolour
REPRODUCED FROM
JOHN UHTHOFF'S SLIDES,
JOY/MICHAEL UHTHOFF
PRIVATE COLLECTION
DIGITALLY RESTORED BY
JANET DWYER

"eliminate the scratched [pots] and other horrors… it was hard to convince the clients that pure form was [something] to be desired."[104] However, the excitement of seeing what would emerge after the kiln was cleared, following a firing, was intense.

Ina's students included Daisy (Dorothy) Bayne Swain, Emily Mae Schofield, Peggy Walton (later Packard, active in the Art Gallery of Greater Victoria) and Betz Sherman Burchett. The latter used pottery as a means to move into sculpture; her salmon swimming upstream won the competition for the entrance of the Alexandra Bridge on the Fraser River.[105] Ina encouraged them to experiment, and Daisy and Emily created "exquisite glazes, a favourite being a blue-green called 'West Wind.'"[106] Peggy had started taking classes with Ina at the old stone house (which she found cold) on Beach Drive. She admired Ina's courage and remembered, "I set to and learned the basics of drawing and painting. Then Ina brought in a bucket of clay and taught us how to sculpt a hand and a mask, showing basic planes. I've been at it ever since."[107]

McNeill Bay near Beach Drive, Victoria, BC, where Ina Uhthoff lived for years,
PHOTO BY AUTHOR, 2012

The school did not appear in the B.C. Department of Education Annual Report in 1938–1939, but the *Victoria Daily Colonist* featured it in a full-page spread in March 1939.[108] Though it mentioned that the school's official recognition by the Department of Education gave it higher prestige, the reputation of Ina Uhthoff as an instructor in her private school carried weight too.

Photographs included the Life Class (showing the students from behind with drawings of the nude model on their easels), the Pottery and Modelling class with eight students and their instructor Ina Uhthoff working with clay, the class of Applied Design, Color and Lettering (lined up working at tables), the Drawing Room with students and Ina facing the camera, the kiln (which had been presented by the City of Victoria to the Pottery Society), an unidentified woman using the potter's wheel and Ina and students with linoleum blocks for making stencils.

The reporter noted:

There flourishes, right in Victoria's midst, one of the most successful adult education projects ever attempted in the West... Students, most of them wearing attractive workmanlike smocks, will be found nearly any morning or afternoon in an attitude of complete absorption at easel, potter's wheel, printer's block, drawing board, designing desk or potter's oven, their earnestness and enthusiasm a silent testimony to the popularity of the studies in which they are engaged.[109]

In the 1939–1940 government report, the Victoria School of Art is well described, including information on the clays and student numbers:

Local and British Columbia clays are used as far as possible, and a distinctive type of Victoria pottery is being established. Because of war conditions, the number of students has shown a decided falling off, but it is hoped that the coming year will show an improvement. The school can offer training in various crafts which should prove of value to those who will have to assist in the rehabilitation of soldiers and others when peace returns to us again. This is the present justification for continuing this school in operation. The enrolment is twenty.[110]

Untitled, n.d., pencil on paper, 8" x 10"
MICHAEL UHTHOFF COLLECTION
PHOTO BY JANET DWYER

In 1940, Ina's school was featured in the IACS's 31st Annual Exhibition, showing the popularity of pottery and clay work: "The Victoria School of Art Kingston Street has a large display of pottery and modeling exhibited under Mrs. Ina D.D. Uhthoff. There are glazed and unglazed pieces with great varieties of design and color, done in a professional manner."[111] John Kyle, just retired from overseeing technical education in B.C., became President of the IACS, where he could foster some support for Ina's school.

What was it like in Ina's classes? Grace Tuckey, who took the Life (drawing and painting) class in 1937, recalled that Ina conformed to standards of decency. Sometimes Grace was the model, pos-

ing in her colourful gypsy costume for twenty-five cents an hour. The showing of nudes, such as Edythe Hembroff's *Nu*, in the Modern Room was rare; conservative tastes still dominated Victoria's art community.

Rosemary Cross, daughter of architect P.L. James, remembered taking lessons from Ina Uhthoff on Kingston Street, as well as later in her studio.[112] The James family lived on Cadboro Bay Road, near Lilian Emerson, her friend and companion in Saturday morning classes. Rosemary recalled her classes and teacher:

> There was usually a model (always clothed)—it would change each week. Mrs. Uhthoff was definitely a "lady." We didn't fool around at all. She would make suggestions by drawing at the edge of your work, never right on your work. She did not touch your work. She would help with drawing such things as how to shape an eye. Sometimes we went outside to sketch by boats but that was rare.[113]

The James family home was filled with art since friends and family members enjoyed painting. Rosemary eventually convinced her parents to buy an untitled oil of a mountain in the Rockies by Ina, one she continued to hang in her own home.

Lilian Emerson (later Rogers) was known for her "Willi Tunes," cartoons of her life in Victoria. One sketch depicted Ina's art class; the teacher was shown with an angry look, blowing smoke, presumably from the cigarette in her left hand. The

Ina Uhthoff Art Class
1946, pen and ink by
Lilian Rogers

model, a bearded logger of European ancestry named Mr. Braur, dressed in a heavy coat, scarf and beret, was visibly sweating and saying, "Ha! I gif you vun minute more! Phew!" Ina, who was known for her "All right" expression, answered, "It's all *right*! *I'm* watching the time, Mr. Braur!"[114] Another student, Margaret Twining, remembered that Lilian rounded up some hefty loggers, who were apt to faint. "One of them had to wear an extremely large fur coat, which could have been his reason. They were not used to posing and remaining still for long periods of time."[115] Another cartoon showed Ina in one of her hats, standing on Yates Street, her legs long and thin. Lilian recalled that she "was a wonderful teacher for me. She knew Lawren Harris, one of Canada's famous Group of Seven, she was a tour de force in Victoria, and the only one with any of training, a hands-off teacher, who respected a person's ability."[116] Lilian described one incident that really inspired her:

> She [took] a blank paper and began moving her pencil randomly on it, making lines in whatever way she felt moved to do. I was fascinated and after she'd gone so far I became so excited that I grabbed the pencil out of her hand and carried on in the same spirit until I thought it was finished. "Well, I guess you've got the idea!" Ina remarked dryly.[117]

For Lilian, "Ina opened the world... She was always there. After the summer, she was keen to see what everyone had been doing. And she was patient with me, even when I got paint on her tweed suit."[118]

Margaret Twining related that Ina was parsimonious in her compliments to her students, usually saying, "Mmmm! Yes" but rarely, "Oh, that's good."[119] Another pupil, Gladys Ewan, called Ina "a treasure. She was so knowing. Mrs. Uhthoff had a basic enlightened training [in Scotland]."[120] Gladys later won the Beatrice Stone Medal at the Vancouver Art Gallery's 1944 Autumn Jury Show, continued to live in

Victoria and worked as a display artist at the University of Victoria's MacPherson Library.

The 1940–1941 government report again included the Victoria School of Art. Although coursework remained the same, particular note is made about the pottery: "A special feature was made of Pottery and Crafts and it is my pleasure to record a decided improvement in the Pottery Section. In several exhibits held throughout the Lower Island the work done by our students has been complimented most highly." The tone of encouragement continued: "The enrolment for full-time courses in the Victoria School of Art has again decreased, but this is compensated for by a larger number taking part-time courses. It is considered that the work done is so valuable that it would be a mistake not to continue to give this opportunity for special instruction to the many gifted young people in the city."[121] Ina Uhthoff no longer listed herself as an Instructor, but again as the Principal of the Victoria School of Art.

Despite Ina's tremendous effort, creating a school full of students was challenging with the advent of World War II. The city was filled with the energy of the armed forces and industry for the war effort. The resurgence of shipbuilding saw the construction of 10,000 ton steel freighters or "Victory ships", mainly at the Victoria Machine Depot (VMD), which built a second yard next to the main Rithet Outer Wharf. At the peak of the war, there would be as many as 3,000 workers on three shifts, seven days a week. Victoria was a busy city, but the focus was not on the fine arts.[122]

According to the 1941–1942 government report, the Victoria School of Art had operated for the full fiscal year but then closed: "The work done by Ina D.D. Uhthoff, the principal of this school, was a decided contribution to the City of Victoria."[123] After that, it was never again listed, though Ina would continue to teach privately and through correspondence courses. She was so well-established that she was included in the 1941 *Who's Who in Northwest Art*.[124]

As Ina's years running her school came to a close and her children graduated from secondary school, a new phase of freedom opened up for Ina, the artist.

‸ *Dutch Canadian,* circa 1945–47, oil on canvas 30" x 24¾"
MICHAEL UHTHOFF
COLLECTION
PHOTO BY JANET DWYER

‸ Label on the back of *Dutch Canadian* for the 16th Annual B.C. Artists' Exhibition, 1947

Muriel worked for a newspaper and as a stenographer for the Canadian Government;[125] John attended university before joining the Royal Canadian Air Force and training as a pilot.[126] Although Ina had experienced the wilds of B.C. in earlier years, drawing and painting the wind-swept beaches and the high mountains that attracted her, now she would have more opportunity to create. While John was stationed near Calgary, she took advantage of this proximity and enjoyed one of her longest sketching and painting trips to the majestic Rocky Mountains—10 months![127] It must have been exhilarating. The many watercolours and oils of Mt. Rundle, Castle Mountain (now renamed Mt. Eisenhower) and other lake, mountain and forest scenes resulted from her trip there.

Ina's paintings have been described by Lorne Render in *Mountains and Sky* as illustrating the "massiveness of the land," conveying "the power of the western landscape" and minimizing "the landscape's elements," while emphasizing "its basic structure and form." It was the simplicity, he wrote, that made her work powerful.[128] The village of Banff, a favourite subject, was shown in different seasons. Ina probably enjoyed fly fishing again. An undated painting of her gear—brown leather bag, full-brimmed hat, curved knife and Cowichan sweater—allude to a more relaxing personal pastime. After an eight-year hiatus, she participated in the B.C. Society of Artists Exhibition at the Vancouver Art Gallery in 1942. The ninety-four artists included Emily Carr, Nan Lawson Cheney, Lawren Harris, Molly Lamb, Max Maynard, Jack Shadbolt, Mildred Valley Thornton, Lilias Farley, B.C. Binning and W.P. Weston. She was clearly in the company of thriving, stimulating artists. Ina also showed in the IACS's 1943 exhibition, garnering comment from the newspapers, which noted that the oil painting section was well-represented with her, John Kyle and others. One article described her painting *Forest Light* as a vivid study in impressionistic style. In another, the reviewer wrote, "Two paintings done at Banff by Ina D.D. Uhthoff, *Beaver Dam* and *Cascade Mountain*, have a lovely posterlike quality."[129]

Untitled (Fishing Gear)
n.d., oil on board
21" x 18", MICHAEL
UHTHOFF COLLECTION
PHOTO BY JANET DWYER

About this time, Ina painted a self-portrait that revealed her technical skill in catching a mood as well as her experimental nature—free brush-strokes and colour highlight the background and her hair (p.43).[130] Her images of First Nations people, possibly done during "Indian Days" ceremonies near Banff in 1942, are different—they are carefully drawn in pencil and charcoal.

After residing for a year on Manor Road, Ina returned in 1944 to the house on Beach Drive with its view of McNeill Bay and the Olympic Mountains. Guy and Eileen Blanchet lived nearby on Mount Joy. The undated painting *Canadian of the North* depicted Guy as the leader of the search party for the MacAlpine party, who had become stranded in the north while looking for potential mines. Later Blanchet told his adventures in the book *Search for the North*.[131]

Banff, n.d., oil on canvas
20¾" x 18¾", FIONA
HERT COLLECTION
PHOTO BY MICHAEL A. COOK

‹ John Campbell Uhthoff,
circa 1942
PHOTO COURTESY OF
NANCY WHITE

‹‹ Muriel Uhthoff, circa
1942, PHOTO COURTESY
OF NANCY WHITE

Canadian in the North (Guy Blanchet), n.d., oil
on canvas, 33" x 31¼", FROM THE ART GALLERY OF
GREATER VICTORIA COLLECTION

~ *Kootenay Mountains,*
n.d., watercolour
REPRODUCED FROM
JOHN UHTHOFF'S SLIDES,
JOY/MICHAEL UHTHOFF
COLLECTION, DIGITALLY
RESTORED BY JANET DWYER

~(*Untitled* (Rocky Mt with
Snag), n.d., watercolour
28" x 20", PRIVATE
COLLECTION

(*Cascade Mountain,*
1943, oil on canvas
22" x 26¾", FROM THE
ART GALLERY OF GREATER
VICTORIA COLLECTION

Teepee, circa 1942, watercolour, JOY/MICHAEL UHTHOFF
PRIVATE COLLECTION

A.M.D. Fairbairn, Esq., 1925, chalk on paper
18½" x 14", NANCY WHITE COLLECTION

First Nation Chief, circa 1942, charcoal
on paper, 29" x 22½", NANCY WHITE COLLECTION

Beach Study, nd., pencil on paper, JOY/MICHAEL UHTHOFF
PRIVATE COLLECTION

Landscape, nd., watercolour on paper
12½" x 15", FROM THE ART GALLERY OF
GREATER VICTORIA COLLECTION

51

FIVE

Artist, Gallery Founder and Columnist

N 1944, INA UHTHOFF WAS LISTED for the *first* time in the B.C. and Yukon Directory as an artist! She maintained a studio at 918 Government Street, where she painted and taught art classes. Peggy Walton, who continued lessons with Ina after the school closed, remembered the upstairs studio being an arty place with a simple hot plate. It was a frigid room, but it was where Peggy got her start as a sculptor. She was offered a bucket of clay and "stayed there until I was congealed with cold."[1] Seeing a painting Peggy did of a cherry tree in full bloom from her front garden, Ina had sarcastically commented, "Ooh! That's the sort of thing I simply hate." Then she added, "You are a natural-born colourist." Peggy loved the painting because it was a symbol of freedom for her and brought back memories of her youth. Though she sometimes found Ina "crusty," all in all, Peggy had great respect for her teacher.[2] Later Peggy taught at Oak Bay Secondary; she and her husband, sculptor David Packard, were strong forces in Victoria's art community.

Portrait of an Artist (A.M.D. Fairbairn) late 1920s, oil on canvas, 27" x 24"
MICHAEL UHTHOFF COLLECTION
PHOTO BY JANET DWYER

›› *Untitled* (Study of Girl Welder), n.d., pastel drawing, 14½" x 16½"
COURTESY OF THE CITY OF BURNABY PERMANENT ART COLLECTION

› *John Uhthoff as Pilot* 1944, pencil on paper
REPRODUCED FROM JOHN UHTHOFF'S SLIDES, JOY UHTHOFF PRIVATE COLLECTION, DIGITALLY RESTORED BY JANET DWYER

› *Girl Welder at Work* 1943, oil on canvas 30½" x 27¼", FROM THE ART GALLERY OF GREATER VICTORIA COLLECTION

Kathleen Metcalf, who later painted with the Victoria Sketch Club, recalled going on Saturdays to Ina's studio in Chinatown between 1945 and 1948. She saw it as cozy with paintings in progress. She also remembered a Russian model with a huge beard.[3] Anne Nolte, another artist with the Sketch Club, studied with Ina at the Wharf Street studio (and later at the Art Gallery).[4] Ina convinced Anne's mother that her daughter would not be happy if she wasn't allowed to go to art school. Hence, Anne attended the Vancouver School of Art and then went to Montreal in 1960 and worked as a secretary for Group of Seven artist Arthur Lismer.

World War II continued to have an effect on Ina and the world around her. After she organized an exhibit in aid of the Red Cross,[5] a newspaper article featured an attractive photo of her in the studio with the painting *Woman Welder* and a portrait of her son as an Air Force pilot.[6] In the photo, Ina is nonchalantly working, garbed in painting smock, with one hand on her hip and the other wielding a brush to touch up the painting. The reporter had expected a temperamental artist; instead, when interrupted in her work, Ina presented with "charm and grace... characteristics which have endeared her to so many Victorians." Her "soft musical voice and the loving way in which she handles her materials" struck the reporter. Ina was known as a "severe critic of her own work. Only faultless drawing satisfies her. Her watercolours are true to the requirements of that medium, simple, translucent and clean." Though capable in many media, she liked oils the best. She considered painting landscapes

Factory Scene, circa
1944, watercolour/
pastel, 22½" x 28½"
IMAGE #PDPO5543
COURTESY OF THE ROYAL
MUSEUM, BC ARCHIVES

to be a form of relaxation, and the same article mentioned that her favourite place to paint was Banff, whatever the season: "She suffered more from horseflies than she did from congealing paints, freezing water, bears, and tourists."[7]

Ina was reported to have gained inspiration from the "virile atmospheres" of the military and shipbuilding workers in Victoria, feeling that the 1940s was not an era of purely beautiful pictures: "These are hard and realistic times which call for strong and vibrant work."[8] She obtained a pass to sketch in the West Coast shipyards, under "the strict injunction not to hinder or impede the performance of duty designated to the furtherance of the war effort." Thus with sketch book and pencil in hand, she spent time "dodging massive cranes, leaping nimbly out of the way of lumbering trucks, keeping her eyes open and trying to keep her ears closed to the deafening roar of the riveters."[9] A wealth of paintings resulted from her experiences in the shipyards, showing workers, boats, cranes and other equipment. Some depict the view from her Wharf Street studio overlooking the Inner Harbour.

> With Canada's entry in WWII had come an urgent need for merchant and
> naval ships. Contracts to build corvettes for the Canadian Navy and freight-
> ers resulted in the building of a second yard which also produced tankers and
> Air Force supply ships. The Victoria Machinery Depot would have been going
> full out.[10]

The paintings of this phase are described as social realism, focusing on workers and working-class activities in a realistic manner.

Ina Uhthoff's *Girl Welder at Work* (and *Woman Welder*)[11] created in various mediums in this period, appeared in the British Columbia at Work series, a 1944

Vancouver Art Gallery exhibit organized by the Labour Arts Guild, a community effort on the part of workers in industry, business and in the various arts.

> It was designed to foster closer co-operation between organized labour and those engaged in advancing the progress of music, fine arts, literature, and drama. The Labour Arts Guild held the conviction that the Labour Movement has need of the artist to give voice, colour, and dramatic emphasis to labour's contribution to the cause of social welfare and national unity. It [was] equally 'convinced that workers in the arts, if they would avoid isolation, futility and the shabby-genteel snobbery, which in recent years has come to be associated with artistic endeavour, must place their talents at the service of the politically and industrially conscious working people.'[12]

The Labour Arts Guild conducted four projects in eight months: People's Concerts on Sunday evenings; Authors' Contests in order to stimulate contemporary Canadian writing of one-act plays, short stories and poems; stage productions of Norman Corwin's "Untitled" radio drama and *Hamlet,* and the British Columbia at Work competitive art exhibition.[13] The latter was unique because it dealt exclusively with the industrial and working life of the province through the media of painting, sculpture,

Untitled (Houses in Woods), n.d., oil on board, 23¼" x 19½"
MICHAEL UHTHOFF
COLLECTION
PHOTO BY JANET DWYER

From Victoria Wharf Street Studio, circa 1944, oil on masonite 18½" x 21¾", IMAGE #PDP04895, COURTESY OF THE ROYAL MUSEUM, BC ARCHIVES

drawing and woodcarving, and also because the trade unions contributed over $600 in cash prizes. Eight paintings (including *Woman Welder*), donated by the artists, were selected from 150 entries to be sent to Vancouver's adopted city, Odessa, to promote the United Nations in the struggle against the forces of Fascist aggression. The presentation of paintings was made possible through the National Council of Canadian-Soviet Friendship in Vancouver. Accompanying the gift of paintings was a hand-lettered and illuminated address of presentation by artist and teacher Grace Melvin of the Vancouver School of Art.[14]

In 1945, Ina bought her first home at 401 Constance Avenue in Esquimalt. It had views over Esquimalt Harbour and across the Juan de Fuca Strait to the Olympic Mountains. Though she would move her studio in the future, she kept this residence for the rest of her independent life. The nearby beach and woods provided the natural subject matter that continually inspired her. Her former student and part-time gardener, David Marryatt, remembered that she liked to paint from a curved window in the attic.[15]

Esquimalt Fair, circa 1950s, gouache on canvas, 10½" x 9½"
MICHAEL UHTHOFF COLLECTION, COURTESY OF MERCURIO GALLERY
PHOTO BY ANDY GRAFFITI

As always, Ina focused her attention on the world around her—adding the industrial scenes to her repertoire. Numerous paintings show working boats and the wharves, as well as pleasure boats at local docks. She depicted different parts of her community, not just Esquimalt—a snow scene in James Bay, Victoria Harbour and a farm scene, probably in nearby Saanich. With breezy, loose brushstrokes, the oil *Esquimalt Fair* shows the Ferris wheel and hamburger stand at an annual local event. Still-life paintings were standard in the classroom; Ina's own still lifes and landscapes became increasingly abstract over the years.

Woods Behind Constance Avenue, circa 1946, oil on canvas, 32" x 23"
JOY UHTHOFF COLLECTION, COURTESY OF MERCURIO GALLERY
PHOTO BY ANDY GRAFFITI

At this time, Ina's son John was stationed in England, where he met Joyce (Joy) Evelyn Turle at a tea dance in Bournemouth.[16] They married in a "blue wedding" on January 14, 1944, at St. Albans Church, where Joy had been christened. Ina was not able to attend, but she did send them a cheque. The couple honeymooned for two

Untitled (Driftwood), n.d.
oil on canvas, 22¼" x 17½"
FIONA HERT COLLECTION

PHOTO BY MICHAEL A. COOK

weeks, and then John was called to military duty, while Joy stayed with her parents. Ina became a grandmother when John Correlli Campbell Uhthoff was born in Bournemouth on January 1, 1945. The following summer, John returned to Canada on the 22,000 ton troopship *Alcantara.*

As a war bride, Joy Uhthoff followed later with baby John on a free but uncomfortable voyage aboard the *Letitia* to Halifax and then by train to Vancouver.[17] Joy was reunited with her husband only briefly, because he was under pressure working on undergraduate courses at the University of British Columbia. She and the baby were sent to Victoria to live with Ina at her Constance Avenue home. It was probably a sad and lonely experience saying farewell once more to her husband and boarding the ferry. Joy recalled her mother-in-law with a friend on the dock, fiddling with beads; she saw them as "two snobby Scots" watching for a war bride. Joy hadn't been able to bathe, but she did have an English tailored suit, so she hoped that she would be presentable.[18] Knowing how close Ina was to her son and what great hopes she had for him, Joy felt the pressure of earning her mother-in-law's acceptance and approval. It was quite a change for Ina to have her grandson and her daughter-in-law living in her home. Though Joy felt that Ina did not find her "classy" enough for her son, she remembered that Ina really loved her grandson, especially when he walked to her. One day John had been crawling; then the next day he stood up and took his first steps towards his grandmother.[19]

About the same time that Joy and the baby arrived, Ina's daughter, Muriel, joined the St. John Ambulance Brigade and was sent to Britain.[20] After taking the train across Canada, she sailed from Quebec City on the *Empress of Scotland* (with twelve women to a cabin) to Liverpool. Mother and daughter stayed in close contact through correspondence, and Ina kept her daughter's letters.[21] Muriel worked for a year as a nurse in Worchester and then was granted a St. John Ambulance Brigade

Scholarship to study physiotherapy. Post-war Britain still had rations, and Muriel had little money as a student, so she was grateful to her mother for sending so many luxuries over the years—cheese, fruitcake, sausages, salmon, soap, powdered milk, Jello, Revlon lipstick and nylon stockings! Her letters tell that her father, Ted Uhthoff, went to Victoria soon after the war, and she hoped he would find a job. He, too, generously sent juice and cookies to his cash-strapped daughter.[22] (Ted had sold the unprofitable fruit ranch and eventually moved to Redfish Creek, spending the winter months in the Sterling Hotel in Nelson.)

Meanwhile in B.C., Joy and the baby finally returned to live with John, while he studied at UBC and worked for B.C. Electric in the summer. With little money, they stayed in the army hut housing for married students, but they visited Ina, especially on summer holidays and at Christmas, when there would be the traditional turkey and plum pudding dinner. Ina's gifts for her grandson would inevitably be something educational, different, and not easily torn up by the baby. Ina did not visit them in Vancouver very much, but she did make the curtains for their army hut home while John finished university. Joy also remembered Ted Uhthoff visiting, showing up unannounced with his backpack. When visiting him in the Kootenays, they stayed in Nelson because his cabin was "too makeshift."

Working life was busy for Ina. Joy remembered her as a "Scot who burned the candle at both ends... always on the cusp of what was happening in the arts."[23] Ina continued teaching art by correspondence[24] (the government also commissioned her to prepare the text for its extension service),[25] as well as maintaining a downtown studio and teaching privately.[26] She painted views from the studio window, one depicting a rainy Victoria street corner near her Broughton Street studio [cover image].[27] She more frequently presented her work in the B.C. Artists exhibitions at the Vancouver Art Gallery: 1945, 1947, 1950 and 1951. She became a member of the B.C. Society of Fine Arts in 1945, exhibiting with them in 1946, 1952 to 1962 and again in 1967.[28] Other artists in these shows included Peter Aspell, Charles Marega, Delisle J. Parker, Gordon Smith, Lionel Thomas, J.W.G. MacDonald, Lawren Harris,

Untitled, n.d., water-colour, 10¾" x 13¾"
MICHAEL UHTHOFF
COLLECTION, PHOTO BY
JANET DWYER

Emily Carr, Alistair Bell, Orville Fisher, Statira Frame and Paul Rand. Some went on to become well-known, while others faded from recognition.

In 1944, Ina's role as a stalwart supporter of a public art gallery in Victoria became more demanding. The Vancouver Art Gallery had been established in 1931,[29] and the idea of one for the capital had been around for decades. In 1932, Emily Carr had proposed a People's Gallery in her home; in 1938, sculptor Katherine Maltwood (and her husband John) had offered to give their impressive art collection to the City and to even build a small hall to house it downtown. All that was requested of the City was operating expenses. It was difficult to convince the municipality and local citizens to support the idea, and nothing had materialized.[30] Katherine Maltwood proved to be a continuing friend of Ina's; they had common interests in supporting the arts and in the mystical, which Ina conveyed in her portrait of Katherine with her sculpture *Canada*. The Maltwoods bought Ina Uhthoff's paintings, which reflected "the great technical versatility of her teaching… fine portraits and a long series of landscapes which capture the moods and rhythms of her physical surroundings [and] possess a silent, bleak, and powerful atmosphere suggesting primeval nature." Among the paintings purchased was *Mount Temple*, in which "rugged and angular mountains are boldly carved in a free palette-knife technique. Using pure colours and little medium, the cool, icy blues of the mountain heights are skillfully set off by a splash of orange and red undergrowth far below." Her more abstract watercolour *Mountain Shadows* comprises "simple, lucid washes, in varying tones of blue, to create stark, monumental forms." Biographer Rosemary Brown summarized:

> In her deep dedication to art Ina D.D. Uhthoff possessed an outspoken enthusiasm and stamina that Katharine Maltwood greatly respected. Their friendship in particular brought the latter into close contact with Victoria's artistic community and its endeavours. Ina Uhthoff's career spans an era of critical awakening in the Victoria art scene.[31]

Now part of the University of Victoria's Legacy Art Gallery, the Maltwood collection contains Ina Uhthoff's work. The Maltwood circle included artist Stella Langdale, who had also trained at the GSA under artist Maurice Greiffenhagen (Ina's favourite instructor there).[32]

The impetus for the successful establishment of a civic gallery was Mark Kearley (son of a viscount), who arrived with his family in 1944 from Switzerland.[33] A war artist with HMCS *Naden* at Esquimalt, he and his family lived in Metchosin. Ina was one of the artists who initially joined him in forming a local branch of the Federation of Canadian Artists (FCA), a national organization (founded in 1941) that would help secure travelling exhibitions.[34] The art gallery movement was officially founded at a meeting on December 8, 1944, with about 50 people in the gymnasium of St. Margaret's School.[35] Since artists from Duncan, Nanaimo and other places were present, they called it the Vancouver Island Region of the Federation of Canadian Artists. Later about 1,000 people met at the Empress Hotel, including representatives of many cultural groups; chief speaker was A.S. Grigsby, Curator of the Vancouver Art Gallery. The next year, a board of directors was formed with Kearley as Chairman and Ina as a member. On July 19, 1946, Viscount Alexander of Tunis officially opened the Little Centre at 965 Yates Street, a building that had been Thomas Plimley's automobile showroom.[36] (With the war, there had been little demand for cars.) The Little Centre had about 300 members, and its leaders envisioned an art centre that encompassed not just the visual arts, but also music and the

atre.[37] Joy remembered that she finally felt accepted by her mother-in-law when she accompanied Ina to the opening of the centre.[38] Ina was on the Display Committee, and the first exhibition, which opened June 1, 1946, featured the work of Emily Carr. Subsequently, the centre sponsored a variety of exhibitions and social events, including the Canadian premiere of the National Film Board's documentary on Emily Carr (held at the Empress Hotel). It also presented the Wedgewood film with a commentary by a descendant of the pottery family who was visiting in Victoria.[39] Lawren Harris and local artist Sophie Deane-Drummond (née Pemberton) also exhibited.[40] In 1947, the IACS held their 38th Annual Exhibition at the Little Centre; Ina contributed her painting *Girl Welder at Work*.[41] The film *West Wind* about artist Tom Thomson was shown at this time. The gallery was trying to incorporate the traditional arts supporters as well as turn eyes to modern trends.

Opening of the Little Centre, July 19, 1946, at Thomas Plimley's Auto Showroom, 965 Yates St., PHOTO COURTESY OF THE *Victoria Daily Colonist*

One of Will Menelaws's students at Oak Bay Secondary helped Ina by hanging pictures and setting up curtains at the Little Centre.[42] He recalled her being middle-of-the-road and "tame" with her art; she was technically excellent, good at drafting and versatile in her media. Strong, tallish, forthright and very definite, she stated her ideas clearly with no equivocation. She could be very supportive: "If you got praise, you knew it meant something. There was no praise for nothing." Volunteers were a key to the operation of the arts centre, and Ina was one of the most consistent contributors of time and expertise over the years.

By 1947, car sales increased, and the fledgling gallery became homeless. The group survived as the Victoria Arts Centre before incorporating as the Arts Centre of Greater Victoria.[43] Kearley's health forced him to resign, and his family returned to

Europe. Bertram Berrick took over as Chairman, and Ina served as Vice Chairman and on the House Committee. The branch then withdrew from the FCA; members deemed the 40 percent of their fees required to belong to be too much.[44]

In 1948, Colonel Casper became President, and Ina again served on the board. In October, an exhibit included her painting *Glacier and Moraine*.[45] The group sponsored a one-week exhibit, featuring 45 of her works, in December 1948 at her 1221 Wharf Street studio,[46] including oil portraits, black and whites, etchings, screen prints and landscapes. Sara Spencer opened the show. Donations collected there were sent to the Food for Britain Fund at city hall.[47] The operation of the arts centre rested almost entirely upon Ina.[48] Colin Graham, past director of the Art Gallery of Greater Victoria, observed that the impetus for establishing the centre was Kearley's European experience and "artist Ina Uhthoff's open-minded acceptance of anything new and vital."[49]

In February 1949, the gallery opened at 823 Broughton Street under the name Arts Centre of Greater Victoria, with the hope that neighbouring municipalities would help with the financing; rent was $75 per month. Architect John Wade did the interior design with swags of material.[50] From 1949 to 1950, Dr. Harry Hickman (President, Victoria College) was President, and Ina headed the Exhibition Committee. At this location the group staged a variety of exhibitions, featuring local, national and international artists, as well as musical events, lectures and films. An announcement of forthcoming exhibitions at the Broughton Street centre for 1950–1951 included Canadian Graphic Arts, Quebec Painters, London Colour Prints, Arthur Lismer, Contemporary British Paintings and Llewellyn Petley-Jones. The centre was under the patronage of the Lieutenant-Governor, the Minister of Education and the Mayor of Victoria.[51]

It must have been heartening for Ina to see her former students exhibiting, such as Lilian Emerson (who humorously cartooned her studio teaching), in the 1950 Non-Jury Show at the Arts Centre. As a reviewer of the 1950 Jury Show reported, "There is an impressive professional appearance to the whole exhibit—not a touch of amateurishness anywhere."[52] Ina contributed two palette-knife paintings, *Harmony in Green* and *A Golden Glow*. With this show, the Arts Centre of Greater Victoria announced that a permanent collection would be started, and recognized Ina D.D. Uhthoff as "a fine artist and tireless worker," when the Executive Committee, under Dr. Hickman, purchased *Sunflowers*, an oil from the Jury Show, for $100 in November 1950. Their plan was to purchase an outstanding work from the Jury Show each year in order to build a representative collection of local painters of artistic and historic value.[53] About the same time, Kearley wrote from Switzerland offering some works of art, and Kathleen and Alexandra McEwen donated their "old masters drawings" and two eighteenth-century Japanese woodcuts.[54] The gallery's permanent collection was starting to grow.

Meanwhile, there were milestones in the personal lives of Ina's family. Muriel continued to study physiotherapy, writing to her mother that she topped the class in anatomy and physiology (noting that 15 out of the 20 students were men).[55] Her letters responded to events in Ina's life, such as the opening and closing of the Little Centre, visiting her sister Edie in Santa Barbara in 1947, recovering from an ankle injury and opening her new studio in 1948.[56] She also kept her mother posted about her friendships and growing love for Trevor Thom, "a curly redhead," who worked for an engineering firm and was "first and foremost a gentleman."[57] Ina still sent her packages, including a black bathing suit; Muriel wrote that it was "so immodest that I can hardly wait for sunshine."[58] Trevor was keen to marry, but Muriel wanted to finish her studies, so they became engaged in February 1948, just before Trevor went to work in Toronto. At last, in June 1949, she passed her final exams and became a member of the Chartered Society of Physiotherapy. On July 23, 1949, Muriel married Trevor Craigie St. Clair Thom at Holy Trinity Church, Forest Row, Sussex.[59] With no immediate family present for a traditional ceremony, Trevor's father, Maurice, "gave her away." Though distance and cost prevented Ina from attending, she was probably pleased to see her daughter complete her course of study and marry well. The couple honeymooned in Paris before settling in Toronto, where Trevor worked for the Steel Company of Canada.

The late 1940s were also a successful time for her son John. In May 1949, he graduated from the University of British Columbia in mechanical engineering (honours).[60] Ina must have been so proud to see his name as the winner under Prizes in Applied Science for the Engineering Institute of Canada's (Vancouver Branch) Moberly Memorial Prize ($25 for books).[61] Soon, however, they moved from the West Coast to King, Ontario, near Toronto and Malton, where John worked for Avro Aircraft, producer of the Avro Arrow, Canada's first supersonic aircraft.

Life in Victoria continued to be vibrant and successful for Ina. Thanks in part to her unflagging energy and support for the Arts Centre of Greater Victoria, the organization survived and thrived to real- ize the dream of a permanent home for the public art gallery. In 1951, board member Sara Spencer, daughter of Welsh department store owner David Spencer, donated the family residence Lan Dderwen, at 1040 Moss Street, as a home for the arts centre.[62] Though some were concerned about the lack of suitable fireproofing (and hence large galleries might not lend original paint- ings for shows), it was realized that a fireproof addition could be added later and that it was time to move forward

with the dream.[63] The president at this time was Ina's friend and colleague Hildegard Wyllie, who with her board took the risk to start operations in the Spencer home, despite the lack of financial commitment from the City.[64]

Like Emily Carr, Ina Uhthoff and her circle aimed to establish a gallery beyond regionalism, where people could see new art that reflected their era: "At its very core, the founding group believed the gallery's mission was to educate the people of Victoria about modernism, allowing the city to take part in the living culture of its time rather than merely revering the past."[65] Ina and her colleagues had seen increased attention to personal expression and the avant-garde in artistic trends. With faster communication and travel worldwide, Victorians were not as iso- lated, as when Ina had first arrived, from movements and groups such as Abstract Expressionism, Colour Field Painting, Lyrical Abstraction, Painters Eleven, Les Automatistes and later Op, Pop, Conceptual and all the extended boundaries of con- temporary art. A strong group of these founding members wanted to exhibit what was current, not just in North America and Europe, but from throughout the world.

A professional curator or director was essential for this move to a permanent home. Convincing Colin Graham to take the job was probably one of the singular most important contributions Ina Uhthoff made to the Gallery. Originally from Vancouver, he was educated at the University of British Columbia and Cambridge University (BA), as well as Stanford University and the University of California at Berkeley (MA).

Untitled (Houses in
Winter), n.d., oil on
canvas, 16½" x 12⅝"
FIONA HERT COLLECTION
PHOTO BY MICHAEL A. COOK

He had taught at the California College of Arts and
Crafts and at the California School of Fine Arts. In
1950, he was the Head of Education at the Legion
of Honor, San Francisco's civic art museum.[66] Colin
knew Vancouver Island, because he had attended
Shawnigan Lake School, and he was familiar with
Victoria, because his parents had retired there.
While visiting his mother, he had taken some watercolour lessons from Ina Uhthoff and enjoyed local
painting and sketching trips with her.[67]

Thus Colin was very interested in moving to
Victoria with his wife Sylvia. In the spring of 1951, he
wrote to Ina to see if she knew of any teaching positions in the Victoria area. Her June reply told him
that she did not know of any teaching positions, but she encouraged him to apply for
the position of curator at the new gallery.

> The Curator's job would be quite varied. He would be in control of the Gallery
> as far as Exhibitions, Lectures, etc… We want someone who is trusted enough
> to build up the Gallery & make it a really live concern. There is a beautiful
> suite of rooms available on the ground floor with its own bathroom. This
> would go with job![68]

Since Colin had no curatorial training, he was honest in communicating that to
Ina, but added that there are many things about the possible curatorship "that I find
stimulating and exciting… I've long had an urge to contribute what such as I could
to raising the quality esthetic [sic] feeling in B.C. and there certainly could be no
more challenging ground than in Victoria."[69] He was clear that he really desired a
teaching job and wanted to be free to accept one if it came up. By August, Colin had
warmed to the idea of working at the Gallery and making it into an alive place with
an imaginative educational focus, "less a staid repository of art objects and more a
vital participating element in community life… [and] make the Gallery something of
a leader among Canadian museums."[70] By September, he accepted the position that
paid him $200 per month plus the suite in the Spencer mansion.[71] A summer 1951
photograph of the board of directors for the Arts Centre of Greater Victoria, standing

outside the new home of the Gallery, showed Ina on the far right, dressed in a business suit.[72] She would continue on the board through 1959, serving as Convener of the Exhibition Committee in 1951 and 1952.[73]

Colin Graham proved to be an exceptional leader, shepherding the Gallery as Curator (the title he preferred), then Director until 1973, when he became Director Emeritus. He and Sylvia (who became a faithful and valuable volunteer) had a continuing friendship with Ina. Sylvia remembered her being kind and gracious, as well as a "real mentor for Colin."[74] Ina would invite them to her home on Constance Avenue, serve them tea and show them her latest paintings. Sylvia recalled that Ina was always experimenting, and there would be a variety of paintings—portraits, landscapes, abstracts. She remembered the house being "spic and span" and a bit chilly until Ina got radiators. The visits were reciprocal, especially after the Grahams moved in 1953 to their new home at the foot of Mt. Tolmie, a barn renovated to a modernist style by local architect John Di Castri.

With Colin Graham secured as Curator, the Gallery moved to establish itself as the Art Gallery of Greater Victoria (AGGV). Though the doors opened to the public in November 1951, the official gala opening occurred almost a year later (October 15, 1952), when Governor General Vincent Massey was available.[75] Colin and his directors knew that they had to educate the public to accept and champion contemporary as well as traditional arts. Thus the opening exhibits featured Quebec Painters, members of the Québécois artistic dissendents Les Automatistes, Jean-Paul Riopelle, Jean-Paul Mousseau and Paul-Emile Borduas, who "shocked" many in the Victoria community, as well as Old Masters that were more familiar to the majority of visitors—the very ones who had the financial means to support the fledgling Gallery.[76]

Though many dismayed letters to the editor were elicited by the rebel Quebec painters, very vehement letters were sent by an anonymous "Man-in-the-Street" and others following the October 1952 Jury Show.[77] They were horrified by the "scrawls, whorls, and indistinguishable masses of color, either brutal or somber… [exhibiting a] complete lack of elementary drawing." In addition, they were irate that so many local artists, who had taken the trouble and expense to frame, hook, wire, label and deliver their paintings, as well as pay the $1 submission fee, were rejected (even in one case, a painting that had been accepted in a previous show). These writers also questioned that jurors (in this case, Ina D.D. Uhthoff) would be allowed to hang some of their work; in their view, jurors should be impartial with no vested interest.[78] This same sentiment about jurors was fermenting in Vancouver, where an "in group" controlled the Vancouver Art Gallery exhibits, and so many artists were excluded, eventually resulting in a February 1958 motion that "no exhibition, selecting or judging committee member, nor his wife or her husband, shall take part in the same exhibition as exhibitor in the Vancouver Art Gallery."[79]

Though obviously seen as unfairly biased from our perspective today, the custom of jurors hanging their own work was not uncommon. Colin Graham wrote a humorous, yet eloquent, response regarding the jury, explaining the reasons and motivations typical for 1952.[80] He took the stance that serving on a jury was difficult, because no jury can satisfy everyone. Ideally, jurors would be called "from the most distant place possible... advised candidly as to local lynching practices; and, when the judging has been done, [be] provided with seats on the next fast plane out of town." The aim of the Gallery was to have three jurors: one who would represent "the traditional and conservative outlook, the other the middle-of-the-road viewpoint, and the third the modern or radical approach." He sensitively pointed out:

> It is a serious and solemn matter to reject the work of a painter who has struggled long and hard and done the best of which he is capable. No juror with elementary humanity feels anything but discomfort with this part of the business.[81]

He clarified that a small gallery such as the AGGV did not have the funds to bring in three jurors from out of town. So they followed the typical practice of asking a member of the Gallery's Exhibition Committee to be one of the jurors. Colin then explained that Ina Uhthoff had "always avoided putting her own work forward as much as she [had] been entitled to while selflessly serving the Arts Centre cause for many years." He pointed out that it was the custom worldwide for jurors, if local artists, to "be invited to contribute two of their own works jury free." Newspaper photographer Ken McAllister also explained the custom of jury show judges being given a complimentary invitation as an incentive because they would have donated many hours normally spent creating their own art. He lamented that it was unfor-

Untitled (Vase, Brushes and Straw Hat), circa 1950s, oil, REPRODUCED FROM JOHN UHTHOFF'S SLIDES, JOY/MICHAEL UHTHOFF COLLECTION DIGITALLY RESTORED BY JANET DWYER

tunate that the small tribute (of allowing her to show her work) was "received so ungraciously" by the anonymous letter writers.[82] Colin concluded his article stating that the Gallery's Jury Show strived to be an exhibition of "work screened by a professional jury whose aim [was] to pick from… submissions a show of the highest possible standards." Ina Uhthoff certainly qualified as a professional with a balanced and critical eye. At the same time, the Gallery President asked the newspaper editor "to cease printing letters to the press written under a pseudonym, especially when attacking personalities."[83]

In order to educate the general public about the Gallery's standards for art worthy of exhibition, Colin invited *Victoria Daily Times* reporter Peter Loudon to the Gallery for a tour with him and the public relations officer. Loudon's self-effacing article described his open-mindedness.[84] With no art training, except a "four-year wartime study of 'pin-ups' in 'mess-deck galleries,'" he thought that he would want to own the still lifes, sea and landscapes because he could readily understand them. However, he could see the value in exhibiting the modern works.

> I did not think I would like to own many of the "self expression" group, the pictures which do not resemble any facet of life seen by the eye. But then, I do not like to eat Brussels sprouts either… which does not detract from their nutritional qualities.[85]

He admired the colour composition in the abstract art and imagined that "if one were to paint a noise it might look like 'this,' whereas a melody might look like 'that.'" Colin Graham had informed him that past artists, whose works are now considered masterpieces, were once criticized. So the reporter concluded that "art lovers, who do comprehend the messages hidden on the art of the new style, are entitled to see it hung in the galleries of the world. They enjoy a language of expression I have not learned."

The debate over what to exhibit, of course, did not end there. Thus the Gallery under Colin Graham's lead put together a strategy to educate and expose the public to modern trends. They developed a fast-paced exhibition schedule so that people would be able to see a wide variety of art from world cultures; there was always something new, which would encourage return visits.[86] It was a beehive of activity with exhibitions, performances, lectures and other events, drawing in people with a panoply of interests and skills. Colin's strength was teaching, and he offered tours of the exhibitions on Friday afternoons, which eventually led in 1959 to the docent program.

Art classes began almost immediately after Colin Graham's arrival. In 1952, Ina closed her downtown studio and began teaching at the AGGV. The long lines outside the mansion on registration day revealed the interest in learning how to create art. Classes took place upstairs; photographs show the students working on the floor of the old Spencer bedrooms until furniture was purchased.[87] Of special interest in November was the "businessman's art course," under Ina's direction.[88] The Gallery was responding to "paint to relax," a "wave of interest that [had] been sweeping Britain and [North America]." It was believed that busy city executives, who doodled during meetings and long-distance phone calls, were seeking an outlet for their artistic souls. Physicians were indicating that a healthy hobby could add years to the life of a harried career man. The class was to be diversified with oils, watercolours,

Study n.d., oil on canvas
24" x 20"
IMAGE #U977.1.23
COURTESY OF UNIVERSITY
OF VICTORIA ART
COLLECTIONS, LEGACY ART
GALLERY, UNIVERSITY OF
VICTORIA ART COLLECTIONS PHOTO

composition, design, landscape, portrait and drawing. The male executive was certainly a lucrative demographic for the Gallery. The many student exhibits over the years built up a viewing public through families, creating ever greater support for the Gallery.

Victoria Daily Times art critic Audrey St. Denys Johnson favourably promoted the classes:

> Earnest, a hard-worker, an idealist in the most practical application of the word, an ardent teacher and a warm friend! These are the honest terms in which one who knows her well may describe Ina D.D. Uhthoff, one of Vancouver Island's leading artists and art authorities.[89]

Audrey had been Ina's student and clearly had positive memories.[90]

Another of Ina's students, David Marryatt, took a Saturday class in the 1950s when he was in his mid-teens.[91] They worked on the staircase and landing of the old mansion, practicing drawing and painting. As he recalled, "Mrs. Uhthoff" let them draw whatever they wanted, calling it "free expression." The girls readily drew flowers, but David was stuck for ideas. He lived near Ina in Esquimalt, and eventually, she gave him a part-time summer job at her Constance Avenue house. He weeded and set stones along the driveway; they had to be set just so or she would get frustrated and be "brisk and to the point." Ina seemed "really old" to him, and though relaxed in some ways, she could be "uptight" if the aesthetics were not just right, making her "fussy." David surmised that Ina thought he would be a better gardener than artist, and soon after he joined the Air Force. Eventually, however, he took education courses at the University of British Columbia, taught industrial arts and enjoyed making sculptural pieces with plastics. Ina's influence may have been stronger than first imagined. As she herself noted, "It takes many years to throw off the influence of a dynamic teacher and find one's own feet and one's own personal expression."[92]

Well-known B.C. artist Michael Morris also took lessons from Ina when he was 12. She gave each student a pad of newsprint and a stick of charcoal and sent them out to sketch the Garry Oaks on the grounds and gave "not much else" in directions.[93] Later he co-founded the Western Front Society in Vancouver and developed a vibrant career as a painter, photographer, video-performance artist and curator. Ina would have been impressed.

In order to promote the Gallery and its programs, Ina agreed in late 1953 to write the exhibition reviews for the *Victoria Daily Colonist*, while Gwladys Downes, teacher and poet, was to write for the *Victoria Daily Times*,[94] though subsequently articles by Colin Graham were more frequently published. Thus began Ina's career as an art critic. Some reviews were merely reporting on what was at the Gallery, giving honest highlights to enjoy or shortcomings to tolerate. Others showed her passion for innovation as well as skillful use of line, colour and other techniques.

Ina always gave attention to student art from the Gallery and the schools; with the newly formed Studio Artists of B.C., she was truthful, yet encouraging when she wrote, "Some of the work is not up to exhibition standard, but it is a movement in the right direction, and we wish them success in their venture."[95] In January 1954, Ina's "Spontaneous Child Art on Exhibit at Centre," advertising the exhibit of work from

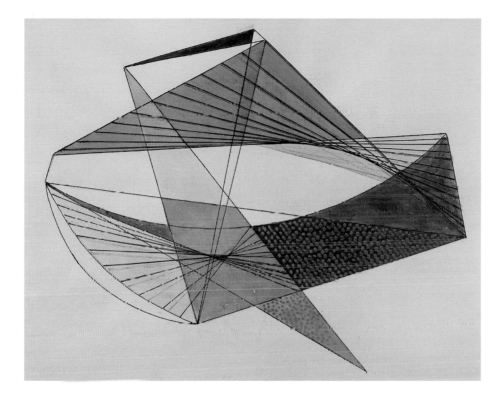

Abstract (1), circa 1952
charcoal, ink and water-
colour, 9½" x 15½"
MICHAEL UHTHOFF
COLLECTION
PHOTO BY JANET DWYER

her children's class, described her observations about child art and reflected why she valued it.

> Drawing is a spontaneous activity in young children, a free expression of their thoughts and experiences. They draw and paint ideas, rather than faithful representation of things, places, and persons. Their mental "images" are extraordinarily clear; they express in line and color what interests them; their concepts are fresh and amusing. Statements are made in untrammeled color and bold line with an authority that many an adult artist might envy. They project their inner world into their pictures.[96]

She noted that a child could complete a large painting in 15 to 20 minutes and rarely overworked it. Ina was also aware (and supportive) of children's different approaches to art—the imaginative child might start right away, drawing an image with complete confidence, whereas another might build up the image from what is observed bit by bit in the environment. Ina was apologetic at the end:

Untitled (Abstract Scene), nd., pastel 24¾" x 21", IMAGE #U977.1.75, COURTESY OF UNIVERSITY OF VICTORIA ART COLLECTIONS, LEGACY ART GALLERY UNIVERSITY OF VICTORIA ART COLLECTIONS PHOTO

Many young people may be disappointed not to find any of their paintings on exhibition, but when one considers that there were so many paintings to be selected from and only a limited amount of wall space available for hanging purposes, one realizes how much good work must be necessarily left out.[97]

Ina, the experienced exhibitor, aware that the show could attract others to her classes, was careful in what was hung. Yet today, with our wide range of tastes and awareness of children's feelings as they develop, one might hesitate to omit a child's work entirely.

Ina was able to analyze what worked and what did not work in an exhibit, yet always kept the article as a vehicle to encourage people to visit the Gallery. In her 1954 review of the Canadian Society of Painters in Water Colour and the Canadian Society of Graphic Artists,[98] she noted that watercolour painting had moved a long way from "the days of the pretty painting, small and of pale hue" because colour was used forcefully, the linear design was clear and texture played an important part. However, she was disappointed that some of the best paintings shown in the east were not in the circuit show. Ina noted that some artists' changing style was disconcerting, but she realized that "an artist cannot remain static. There is always the striving for development in new ways."

Ina's reviews reflected the eclectic vision of the Gallery. There were traveling exhibits from the National Gallery of Canada and other institutions, as well as locally created shows. Among the exhibits Ina reviewed were 20th Century American paintings (Winslow Homer and others), eastern Canadian painters (David Milne, Tom Thomson), Yousef Karsh photographs, Northwest Coast Indian carvings, British Watercolours, Contemporary Graphics, Japanese Wood Block Prints, Eskimo Sculpture, Tarascan (Mexico) Sculpture, Master Drawings of Four Centuries, Korean Ceramics and Picasso Etchings. She found the Latin American Painting (especially Mexican Diego Rivera, Jose Orozco and David Alfaro Siqueros) one of the most impressive exhibitions ever shown there.[99] She remarked that the expressionist paintings (Vlaminck, Pissarro, Chagall, Dufy, Utrillo and others) of a 1956 European Masters exhibit were undoubtedly most important because they did so much "to free painting from limitations of the Victorian era"; she noted that "our eyes... have become somewhat accustomed to crude color used by less mature contemporary painters, [but there is] a rich sobriety in these European works."[100]

Ina gave strong support to B.C. artists, including innovator Emily Carr, traditionalist Sophie Deane-Drummond and Vancouver artists Bruno and Molly Lamb Bobak. It must have been a pleasure for her to review the solo show of her long-time colleague and fellow Scot Will Menelaws, called by some the "Dean of Victoria artists." Ina brought attention to the fine draughtsmanship and freshness of the washes in his paintings *Inner Harbour, Japanese Training Ship* and *Abandoned*, though she preferred *Street in Tacoma*.[101] Ina had only positive comments for a show of B.C. Arts, conceived by Tony Emery in 1956.[102] Featuring contemporary artists from Vancouver and Victoria, it included paintings, pen-and-ink drawings, graphic arts, ceramics and silversmithing. Ina found the work of Victoria painters Margaret Peterson, Herbert Siebner and Jan Zach to be outstanding, and she commented on the "acutely sensitive vision" in the intimate painting of Myfanwy Pavelic (niece of Gallery donor Sara Spencer). More than once, she wrote about Jan Zach and his students' work; she described his sculptures, paintings and "contructivist" work as having immense vitality.[103] She was also complimentary about the watercolours of Fred Amess (when he was director of the Vancouver School of Art) and the late-in-life work of John Kyle, who had been so important in helping Ina establish her career in Victoria.[104] By featuring local artists, the Gallery built rapport with the community. One exhibition that limited the subject matter to Victoria's Inner Harbour drew 80 paintings from a variety of artists, including Herbert Siebner and his students (such as Nita Forrest and Molly Privett), Isobel Hobbs and Will Menelaws.[105] For the Vancouver Island Jury Show of 1958, Ina noted fewer entries but higher quality, and she wrote again about the work of Herb Seibner, as well as a relative newcomer, Richard Ciccimarra.[106]

As newspaper writer for the Gallery, Ina continued to educate the public about looking at modern art with an inquiring mind. She herself created more abstract works as she grew older. She was forthright in her review of the Quebec Automatistes in 1957.[107] "Yes, it is framed, it is a picture! The artist is trying to achieve immensity and lyric abstractness by painting white upon white," she explained to potential Gallery visitors, gazing with puzzled expressions, at a painting of white with a faint underglow of yellow. She encouraged them to accept non-objective painting without prejudice and to try not to identify objects in the painting. The way a picture was painted, not the subject, was of importance with this kind of art, because these artists were drawing upon the subconscious mind. "The test of a painting is whether it has anything to say. In this group much is being said in a spontaneous and stimulating manner."[108] Ina loved the work of Gordon Smith, whom she found to be a person of great sincerity and modesty: "There are no 'tricks' in his work; it follows a logical course of search, often verging on the abstract but always turning to the source of nature for fresh stimulus."[109] She noted that, though his rocks might not look like rocks, it must be admitted that the beauty of shapes "more than justified his free use of them as a starting point from which to build his harmonies of lusciously used paint."

Though usually very positive about experimentation and challenging boundaries in contemporary art, Ina had a standard of quality, which was expressed most emphatically in a review of the 1958 exhibit of New York painters.

> The freshness and power of American painting have created for it an established position in contemporary art. But I do not feel that the collection of the work of New York painters at the Art Gallery this week adds anything to this prestige. At first glance, the paintings appear to possess that valuable and essential quality of spontaneity. Vigor is apparent in almost all the work, but is that enough? Should it not be controlled by idea? Because colors are sloshed around on a canvas we are not necessarily witnessing an eruption of spontaneous expression. When we are offered smears of paint and little else, we become bored. We look for refinement of form and texture and a visible deliberation in the design.[110]

Though she followed her custom of saying positive comments about the show, Ina's lament was remarkably different from her pleas to look without negativity at newer art, which challenged one's idea of what was good. Months later, she reviewed an exhibit of contemporary British paintings, again questioning the directions of the modern art world.

> Artists, all over the world, are going through a difficult time. There is no longer any tradition by which to guide one's development, there are too many

opposing points of view. Craftsmanship is no longer of much consequence; it may be adequate but must not be assertive. So often it is not adequate. A good deal of the work in this collection reflects this spirit of uncertainty.[111]

As Ina grew older with her decades of perspective, she saw a changed world whose creations did not necessarily adhere to her standards, even broadly, and whose directions were unclear.

In her newspaper articles, Ina astutely gave support to existing and potential donors. There was good coverage of a City Collectors Show (with works from private homes) in 1956.[112] The 1957 gift to the Gallery from H. Mortimer Lamb of drawings, paintings, etchings and wood engravings enriched the growing permanent collection.[113] Ina's former teacher Mark Tobey donated works to the Gallery, forming a nucleus of an all-American collection of high-ranking contemporary art.[114] Not only was the Gallery actively building up their own collection, it was building support for the fireproof additions. In 1956, Clark and Pickstone's plans for the addition won the $250 prize in the Rotary-sponsored design contest, and an anonymous donor had pledged $5,000 to open the drive for funds.[115] The Gallery expanded the opportunities for citizens to be involved with art by initiating the Picture Loan program in 1957, so that art could be enjoyed and contemplated in homes or offices.

In 1958, it was no surprise that Ina Uhthoff's *Sunflowers* was included in the 100 Years of B.C. Art at the Vancouver Art Gallery to mark British Columbia's centennial. Ian McNairn, in writing about contemporary painting and sculpture, certainly reflected the value of Ina Uhthoff's work.

> We must... remember that personality has an important effect on the artistic temperament—the effect of the teacher's personality on his pupils and the artist's personality on his public. In both these aspects, the vitality of British Columbian art owes much to the teachers of the present generation of leading artists, and can also take heart for the future. In some cases, the personality can be seen in the style of pupil's art but often what is more important is the contagious germ of enthusiasm for what is being done, the technical assurance, and artistic integrity.[116]

Along with many of her colleagues, Ina's dual role as artist and teacher was continuing and clearly acknowledged here.

SIX

The Last Decade

B Y 1962, THE ART GALLERY OF GREATER VICTORIA was well-established, and Ina Uhthoff was a highly respected leader in the arts, even though she had done less teaching and exhibiting for ten years. She had been devoted to serving the Gallery and working as the *Victoria Daily Colonist* art critic at the expense of her own painting. However, in April she had a solo exhibition at the Gallery, showing her work from the past decade. Though one reviewer observed that some compositions were abstract or non-objective, Ina's firm belief that an artist should start from nature, allowing it to express itself, shone more prominently. Colin Graham found that her gouache *After Snow* revealed that there is "probably no painter in this province who grasps more instinctively the natural properties of this particular medium with its potentialities of both transparencies and opacity."[1] Also in the show was the large oil *Looking Down* of rooftops and portraits, *Old Man* in black chalk and *Self Portrait*, an oil with a Fred Varley-like quality. Her oil painting *Suburbia*, also drawn from

《 *Untitled* (Rooftops), n.d.
watercolour on paper
23½" x 18", NANCY
WHITE COLLECTION
PHOTO BY NANCY WHITE

81

Untitled (Arbutus Tree)
n.d., oil on canvas
12½" x 15½"
FIONA HERT COLLECTION
PHOTO BY MICHAEL A. COOK

the rooftop subject matter, was purchased by the Greater Victoria Teachers' Association and presented to the University of Victoria. Her work was considered an inspiration and an example of a top-flight artist in Victoria.[2]

In 1963, Ina had a show at the Reference Library in the Parliament Buildings. Fellow artist Maxwell Bates, in his review, considered it one not to miss.[3] He recognized her skill in drawing, which was "not always true of artists in our time," as well as her insight. He warned visitors to look carefully, for "much could be missed by a casual observer." Bates was aware of the changing times, when the value of a sound grounding in drawing and other skills could be overlooked in a world giving its greatest attention to non-objective art and emotional expression.

Throughout the 1960s, Ina continued to teach the correspondence course and to write for the *Victoria Daily Colonist.* Her reviews of Englishmen George Baxter's colour prints and German expressionist Ernst Barlach's lithographs again show the Gallery's access to a wide variety of works. Ina was particularly moved by Barlach's work, especially his *Self-Portrait* where she found a "face of one who looks on tragedy, the penetrating eyes of one who understands and feels the sorrows of mankind." His *Three Gray Women* claimed her attention with "the drawing of gnarled hands, the expression of age and poverty in the shapeless coverings or the claw-like toenails of the old woman" that aroused her pity.[4] Ina could recognize moving pathos communicated through recognizable subjects drawn with skill.

When reviewing Some Painters of the B.C. Mainland, organized by the Gallery in 1966 with Canada Council support to commemorate the centenary of the union of the colonies of Vancouver Island and British Columbia, Ina noted "some violent work and a good deal of experimentation," but she found it alive and stimulating overall. However, she concluded, "At all costs, let there be vitality! But one sometimes wonders what and where all that vitality is going to lead. Let us hope that it will be of lasting significance."[5] In a review of pop art (Roy Lichtenstein, Andy Warhol and others), which she expected to be noisy and somewhat vulgar, she surprisingly found restraint

and a dignity of approach: "Each artist has plenty to say that is stimulating and different."[6] However, her opinions about an op art exhibit drew negative criticism.

> What I find lacking in op art [is] personal vision. The technique is there, but why should it be hailed as New Art? There is nothing new about it, beyond a reaching out for a wider range of materials... it does not draw one back. One passes it over to go to more vital things. It should really be classed as commercial art as it has been taught in art schools for at least half a century now.[7]

In the same article, she praised the Women's Committee Cultural Fund's exhibition, which featured works they had purchased. Ina found it to be one of the most comprehensive and interesting of the year: "We may have seen some of the items before, but there is no feeling of repetition, as a good painting or drawing gives out more each time one sees it."[8] One of her favourite artists was Canadian David Milne, especially his *Black Reflections, Bishop's Pond*. She found him completely uninfluenced by

Suburbia, n.d., mixed media, 25¾" x 29¾"
IMAGE #U977.1.73
COURTESY OF UNIVERSITY OF VICTORIA ART COLLECTIONS, LEGACY ART GALLERY
UNIVERSITY OF VICTORIA ART COLLECTIONS PHOTO

Abstract Rooster, nd.
watercolour, 13½" x 17"
NANCY WHITE COLLECTION
PHOTO BY NANCY WHITE

any current trend: "He created something that had not been done by any Canadian painter, a new outlook with the simplest material, by temporarily cutting himself off from conflicting influences in order to develop fully his own personal vision."[9]

Ina, who worked away diligently in Victoria and did not indulge in fireworks to promote herself on the national and international scenes, was probably dismayed at what contemporary artists were doing to get attention. "Painting cannot remain static; it must venture forth seeking fresh means of expression, but I claim that it should know where it is going. Much of this painting does not appear to do so. There is too much striving to impress."[10]

Ina wrote her columns out by hand, which led to some embarrassing situations when they were transcribed.

> I am not able to type, consequently what I write has to pass through several hands before it is published and many errors creep in which are often disastrous to meaning or structure. There was a bad one recently on Toni Onley's show at the university and there were three misprints in the recent one on Mrs. Irwin's (the well-known poet P.K. Page) exhibition at the art gallery. It

Portrait of a Chinaman
(Mr. Wong), 1960, oil
on canvas, 22" x 18¼"
COLLECTION OF THE
VANCOUVER ART
GALLERY, ACQUISITION
FUND, VAG 94.10.9
PHOTO: TIM BONHAM,
VANCOUVER ART GALLERY

appears to happen in the typesetting. This has been going on for a long time
now. My reviews go to the National Gallery of Canada and to many of the
leading American art galleries.[11]

In 1968, Ina seemed to have come to some resolution about modern trends and
how to value them when the Royal Canadian Academy exhibit was shown at the
Gallery. The large show of 85 works included painters of representational subject

matter, avant-garde painters working along experimental lines and sculptors in metal, wood and cement.

> There is little that is dull in this show; some of it is shatteringly upsetting. We find it hard to recognize the most recent contributions of some of our favourite painters... But it creates plenty of controversy, and that is all to the good. We are living in an age of violence and need not be shocked to find it coming out in contemporary art. It is better than being bored by large and showy canvases of layouts reminiscent of first year art school design or elementary pattern making. They cover wall space but have little to say. Manual dexterity is their chief distinction. Nature does not exist for this group of painters but they are strong on rhythm and that after all is more important than cramping one's style by trying to reproduce visual experiences in paint.[12]

Ina's concern for quality of the past being lost in the modern trends was expressed as she reviewed an exhibit on portrait painting. It was one of her great strengths, which she felt was less and less appreciated as she aged, observing that portrait painting was, to a great extent, out of favour at that time.

> The modern home does not always provide a suitable setting for works of any size, but one feels that a great deal of the dignity and tradition of family life may be going. Not only that, but we have few top-ranking portrait painters in Canada now.[13]

Throughout the 1960s, Ina continued to nurture younger artists who arrived on the scene. Well-known B.C. printmaker and arts advocate Pat Martin Bates moved to Victoria in December 1963 with her husband (who was in the Canadian Forces) and two children. She recollected how Ina "took her under her wing." As neighbours in Esquimalt, they spent "many hours looking at her art books and talking the talk."[14] When Pat had her first show in the archives gallery, she was grateful for Ina's review in the newspaper. Ina championed a variety of artists through her articles, including promoting the annual sale of local artists' work by the Women's Committee, which raised valuable funds for the Gallery and supported both emerging and internationally known artists.

Ina realized that she could not keep up her usual pace, especially when tired from seasonal illnesses. She also almost had an accident driving her VW bug off a ramp into the sea at Clover Point.[15] The May-June 1969 "Art Gallery of Greater Victoria News" announced that she had tendered her resignation from her gallery responsibilities. They responded by appointing her a member of the Honorary Advisory Board, calling her the "doyen of Victoria painters."[16] Ina's family had concerns about her living independently on Constance Avenue, so they urged her to move to a small apartment; she had apparently left the stove on and fallen down when a fire started.[17] Without the steady responsibilities of her career, she planned to go east, where her son and daughter were living. "I'm longing to come to you all, the loneliness is just too much. I was stupid to resign from all the art gallery committees, but after I had the flu, I was completely pooped, and my memory went on turning somersaults."[18]

Ina went to live in the guest room at 10 Jenckes Street, a restored heritage house that was home to Muriel, her husband and two daughters, Nancy and Fiona, in Providence, Rhode Island.[19] When Muriel and Trevor went on a business trip to Florida, Ina stayed in the family home with the two girls, though a paid helper was needed to monitor them all. Nancy recalled that her grandmother was interested in her art and gave her honest critiques.[20] Though she liked having Ina there, she found it hard to come home from school to find her mother and grandmother—two strong women—at "loggerheads." At one point, Ina had packed her bag and was walking out of the house.[21] Muriel tried to get her an apartment down the street, but Ina preferred Victoria. Muriel wrote, "She is most secretive as far as I am concerned. I represent AUTHORITY which she is bucking madly and for this she cannot be blamed. She has great lucid moments and then others which are extremely childish."[22] Muriel lamented:

> She is desperately homesick and longs to return to Victoria which is understandable. My brother and I are in a quandary about her future. She feels imprisoned here but is living life to the full. Is there any way she can live and not just exist in Victoria? She feels that she has a place in Victoria.[23]

While in Rhode Island, Ina wrote about her life. She had collected extensive records of local art events, but these documents were in Victoria. However, she wrote

Untitled (Boats in Harbour), circa 1960s watercolour, 9½" x 13"
MICHAEL UHTHOFF
COLLECTION
PHOTO BY JANET DWYER

what she could remember, hoping to access her collection later for a book, which would be a comprehensive survey of the arts in the capital city, starting in 1922. She modestly stated, "I'm afraid that I may be obliged to put myself more prominently in the picture than I would like."[24] Her notes and some news clippings are now with the AGGV. Muriel wrote to Colin Graham that Ina's work on the history came in fits and starts and that Muriel would type up what she could salvage.[25] In 1970, Ina wrote to him about her experiences, which kept her interest as the months seemed to "drift away meaninglessly" in Rhode Island.[26] Ina was not happy in the U.S. and very homesick: "I hate the place. I want to be back on Canadian soil and back to my book in Victoria."[27] She longed to be home on Constance Avenue with the woods of Saxe Point nearby and the view of Juan de Fuca Strait. She had watched the changing sea and sky, including an unusual vision of Venus—five green lights in a row with a red light above. She was quoted in the newspaper, "I could hardly believe my eyes because there it was, hanging in space."

Muriel wrote to Colin about her mother, "She relies on your opinion more than she will ever admit to you... Mother watches the mail daily and longs for news from the Art Gallery."[29] In 1970, John wrote of making arrangements for his mother to live in the Mt. Baker Apartments on Newport Avenue, near her former homes in Oak Bay. Her excess furniture was to go to Kilshaws Auction, and the mortgage payment for the Constance Avenue home was to still go to the Bank of Montreal. However, the Directory listed her living at 1065 Oak Bay Avenue.[30]

In February 1971, Ted Uhthoff died at the age of 85 at the Kootenay Lake District Hospital in Nelson, B.C. A service was held and the Death certificate showed he was still married to Ina.[31]

John was quite worried about his mother living alone, and by 1971, Ina had gone to live with his family in Ottawa (wife Joy, sons John and Michael). It was a difficult time for all—the boys had to share a bedroom, to free one for their elderly grandmother. After such an independent life, she felt uncomfortable having less control of her life, and so she appeared dictatorial and demanding.[32] Ina eventually moved to a nursing home, Carlton Place in Ottawa, where on June 29, 1971 at age 81, she passed away. Funeral services were held at McCall Brothers Floral Chapel in Victoria, with interment at the Royal Oak Cemetery.[33]

Untitled (Winter Scene and Fence), n.d., water-colour on paper 10¾" x 11¾", NANCY WHITE COLLECTION
PHOTO BY NANCY WHITE

In recognition of Ina's tremendous legacy as an art critic, teacher and artist for almost 50 years in Victoria, and most importantly for her contributions to the formation of the AGGV, the Gallery organized a memorial exhibition featuring her art in February and March 1972. Long-time friend and colleague Colin Graham wrote the catalogue, praising a capable woman whom he knew Victoria should not forget. He wrote to John Uhthoff, who had not been able to attend:

> The general reaction to the show would, I think, certainly have warmed your heart. It was happily one of those rare exhibitions which everyone without exception liked and admired. Many people were more than a little astonished to find out what a very strong artist your Mother had been.[34]

Colin knew the value of Ina's work and gently communicated with her son and daughter as they went through the process of grieving their mother and deciding where her works of art (over 400) would go. Muriel and her family kept a share, which is still largely intact. John and his family put many of their paintings up for sale. Though Ina's work comes up for sale at galleries and auctions, the family arranged for a number of her quality paintings and prints to stay with the gallery she loved.[35] After his mother died, John began the meticulous task of documenting his mother's art. He knew that her life had been important to Victoria's artistic success and heritage and wanted to preserve her memory for future generations. John photographed her art and kept notes that have been valuable to the research of this book. A few slides have been restored. Forgotten pieces attest to Ina's drive to create all her life.

Meanwhile, her artistic abilities have been carried on by her grandchildren. Nancy Thom White completed a BFA at the San Francisco Art Institute and is presently a freelance graphic and web designer in the Boston area. Her older sister, Fiona Thom Hert, a dean at Grand Rapids Community College in Michigan, earned her BA in art history from New York University, and then worked for Ford Foundation's Centre for Native American Arts in Anchorage, Alaska.[36] Grandson Michael Trevor Uhthoff is a fine furniture designer/builder in the Victoria area who loves boating and fishing. His older brother, John Correlli Campbell Uhthoff, was an inventor, guitarist and one of the CBC's top sound technicians. He ran his own electronics business, Cinetronics, and was sent on many trips by the CBC with Pierre Trudeau and Rene Levesque. He passed away early in 2012. Michael now advocates for his grandmother's art and has assisted in coordinating a few exhibitions in Victoria. One notable comment he made during the research for this book was that his grandmother was very critical of her own work and threw a lot away. He felt she would only be happy if just her best art was recorded for posterity. She was a proud Scot with high standards to the end.

In the Memorial Exhibition catalogue, Colin Graham described how Ina Uhthoff's professional expertise had charted a sound artistic course and kept operations at a respectable level of quality. The whole project of establishing the Gallery may have collapsed if Ina had not given her services "unstintingly, tirelessly, and constantly." To do so, she gave up time for her own painting and income from teaching. Yet Ina claimed that the happiness of her activities with the Gallery greatly outweighed the value of any services she had given.[37] He also identified a chief characteristic that had ensured her personal success as well as that of the Gallery.

INA D. D. UHTHOFF

MEMORIAL EXHIBITION

Memorial catalogue cover, Art Gallery of Greater Victoria, 1972
COURTESY OF THE BURNABY ART GALLERY

What strikes one as remarkable, when one considers her lack of opportunity to travel abroad and the extreme conservativeness of the Victoria environment, is the open mind with which she received and endorsed with enthusiasm, the various forms of abstract art… she consistently welcomed the new whenever it had quality.

Ina D.D. Uhthoff in director's chair, circa 1960s, PHOTO COURTESY OF NANCY WHITE

Yes, Ina Uhthoff was an artist with excellent observation skills, discerning taste and impeccable judgement. Like an astute and patient fly fisher, she could sense the pace and play the angles to land the prize. In Victoria she was in the right waters and knew her depth. Ina Uhthoff was a determined doer who made things happen where they had never happened before—most notably an art school and a permanent public gallery in Victoria. For this she should not be forgotten.

INA D.D. UHTHOFF

EXHIBITIONS

Untitled (Kitchen Table)
circa 1945–50, oil on
canvas, 18" x 21"
PRIVATE COLLECTION
REPRODUCED FROM JOHN
UHTHOFF'S SLIDES, JOY/MICHAEL
UHTHOFF COLLECTION, DIGITALLY
RESTORED BY JANET DWYER

1911   Royal Glasgow Institute of Fine Arts

1912   Royal Glasgow Institute of Fine Arts

1912   Royal Scottish Academy

1913   Royal Glasgow Institute of Fine Arts

1916   Royal Glasgow Institute of Fine Arts
Royal Scottish Academy

1917   Ralph Proud Gallery, Glasgow, solo exhibition

1925   16th Annual Exhibition of Painting, Drawings, Designs, and Crafts, Island Arts and
Crafts Society (IASC), Art Gallery, Crystal Gardens, Victoria

1926   17th Annual Exhibition of Paintings, Drawings, Designs, and Crafts, IASC, Victoria

1927   18th Annual Exhibition of Paintings, Drawings, Designs, and Crafts, IASC, Victoria
Annual Fair, Willows Fairground (organized under the auspices of the IASC), Victoria

1928   19th Annual Exhibition of Original Paintings, Drawings, Designs, and Crafts, IASC,
Belmont Building, Victoria
Canadian National Exhibition, Toronto

1929   21st Annual Exhibition", B.C. Society of Fine Arts B.C. Art Gallery, 649 Seymour Street,
Vancouver

1930   Canadian National Exhibition, Vancouver
21st Annual Exhibition of Paintings, Drawings, Designs, and Crafts, IASC, Board of
Trade Building, Victoria

1931   22nd Annual Exhibition of Paintings, Drawings, Designs, and Crafts, IASC, Victoria

1932   23rd Annual Exhibition of Paintings, Drawings, Designs, and Crafts, IASC, Belmont
Building, Victoria

1933 24th Annual Exhibition of Paintings, Drawings, Designs, and Crafts, IASC, Belmont House, Victoria

1934 25th Annual Exhibition of Paintings, Drawings, Designs, and Crafts, IASC, Victoria
B.C. Artists 3rd Annual Exhibition, Vancouver Art Gallery

1935 26th Annual Exhibition of Paintings, Drawings, Designs, and Crafts, IASC, Belmont House, Victoria

1936 27th Annual Exhibition of Paintings, Drawings, Designs, and Crafts, IASC, Victoria

1939 Vancouver Island Exhibition (IASC), Vancouver Art Gallery

1940 31st Annual Exhibition, IASC, Victoria

1942 B.C. Artists 11th Exhibition, Vancouver Art Gallery

1943 34th Annual Exhibition, IASC, Crystal Gardens, Victoria

1944 Artist's studio, solo exhibition, Victoria
B.C. at Work, Labour Arts Guild, Vancouver Art Gallery

1945 14th Annual Exhibition, British Columbia Artists' Exhibition, Vancouver Art Gallery
Artist's studio, 918 Government Street, solo exhibition, Victoria

1946 Artist's studio, 534 Broughton Street, solo exhibition, Victoria
36th Annual Exhibition, B.C. Society of Fine Arts, Vancouver Art Gallery

1947 38th Annual Exhibition, IASC, Little Centre, Victoria
16th Annual Exhibition, British Columbia Artists Exhibition, Vancouver Art Gallery

1948 37th Annual Exhibition, IASC, Arts Centre, Victoria
Arts Centre of Greater Victoria
Arts Centre of Greater Victoria, solo exhibition at artist's studio, 1221 Wharf Street

1950 19th Annual Exhibition, Jury Show, British Columbia Artists Exhibition, Vancouver Art Gallery
Arts Centre of Greater Victoria, Jury Show

1951 20th Annual Exhibition, Jury Show, British Columbia Artists Exhibition, Vancouver Art Gallery

1952   42nd Annual Exhibition, British Columbia Society of Artists, Vancouver Art Gallery

Art Gallery of Greater Victoria, Jury Show

1953   43rd Annual Exhibition, British Columbia Society of Artists, Vancouver Art Gallery

1954   44th Annual Exhibition, British Columbia Society of Artists, Vancouver Art Gallery

1955   45th Annual Exhibition, British Columbia Society of Artists, Vancouver Art Gallery

1956   46th Annual Exhibition, British Columbia Society of Artists, Vancouver Art Gallery

1957   47th Annual Exhibition, British Columbia Society of Artists, Vancouver Art Gallery

1958   48th Annual Exhibition, British Columbia Society of Artists, Vancouver Art Gallery

100 Years of B. C. Art, to mark British Columbia's Centennial Year, Vancouver
    Art Gallery

1959   49th Annual Exhibition, British Columbia Society of Artists, Vancouver Art Gallery

Portfolio of Prints of Eight Artists

1960   50th Annual Exhibition, British Columbia Society of Artists, Vancouver Art Gallery

1961   51st Annual Exhibition, British Columbia Society of Artists, Vancouver Art Gallery

1962   52nd Annual Exhibition, British Columbia Society of Artists, Vancouver Art Gallery

Art Gallery of Greater Victoria, solo exhibition

1963   Reference Library, Parliament Buildings, solo exhibition, Victoria

1967   57th Annual Exhibition, Centennial Year, British Columbia Society of Artists,
    Vancouver Art Gallery

1972   Memorial Exhibition, Art Gallery of Greater Victoria

Ina Uhthoff: 1889–1971, Grand Forks Art Gallery, solo exhibition, included works
    between 1912–1943

1979   DeVooght Gallery, solo exhibition, 2215 Granville Street, Vancouver

1981   The Modern Room (recreation of the 1932 exhibition), Emily Carr Gallery, Provincial
    Archives of British Columbia, Victoria

1982   Art from the Gallery's Collection, Art Gallery of Greater Victoria

1983   Printmaking in British Columbia 1889–1983, Art Gallery of Greater Victoria

1985   Women Artists 1885–1985, Art Gallery of Greater Victoria

1990   Ina Uhthoff: the Early Years, solo exhibition, organized by The Gallery, Travellers' Block Annex, 28–3rd Avenue, Saskatoon, Saskatchewan

1991–92   Ina Uhthoff: The Early Years, solo exhibition, Medicine Hat Museum and Art Gallery, Alberta

1995   Early British Columbian Women Artists, Heffel Gallery, Vancouver
Ina Uhthoff: Drawings, Water-Colours, and Oils from the 1920s to the 1950s, solo exhibition, The Gallery, Travellers' Block Annex, Saskatoon, Saskachewan; also at the Glenbow Museum, Calgary, Alberta

1996   Canadian Women Artists, Winchester Galleries, Victoria

2002   Paintings from the Estate of Ina D. D. Uhthoff, Winchester Galleries, Victoria

2010   Emily's Revenge: More Victoria Modernists, Mercurio Gallery, Victoria

2011   Mercurio Gallery, solo exhibition, Victoria

2011–12   Autobiography of a Gallery, Vancouver Art Gallery

Untitled (Kokanee Glacier), n.d., oil on board, 16" x 28"
MICHAEL UHTHOFF COLLECTION, PHOTO BY AUTHOR

PUBLIC COLLECTIONS

Art Gallery of Greater Victoria

Burnaby Art Gallery

B.C. Archives

Glenbow Museum

University of Victoria Legacy Art Gallery

Vancouver Art Gallery

PRIVATE COLLECTIONS

Canada, USA, Scotland

ACKNOWLEDGEMENTS

Warm thanks to the artist's family who provided so much original material and enthusiastically supported the book. To John Uhthoff's wife Joy Uhthoff and to Ina's grandson, Michael Uhthoff who told me stories and showed me her art. To Ina's granddaughters by her daughter Muriel Thom: Fiona Hert and Nancy White. Special thanks to Nancy, who hosted me in Massachusetts, fueling me with a delicious meal and interesting talk, so that I could be up the whole night reveling in Ina Uhthoff's art.

The following galleries/museum institutions were immensely helpful with the preservation of the artists' works and papers and for the above-and-beyond assistance given to me. The Art Gallery of Greater Victoria gave me space, use of equipment and on-going patience with questions. Thanks go to Mary Jo Hughes (Curator), Lori Graves (Registrar), Stephen Topher (Special Collections), Marie-Andree Furlong (IT Administrator), and Judy Thompson (Archivist). At the Vancouver Art Gallery I received great assistance from Kristen Fung (Curatorial Staff), Susan Sirovyak (Registrar) and Cheryl Siegel (Library/Archives). At the British Columbia Archives my longtime colleague Katherine Bridge told me about this project and answered a million questions. Thanks go also to the Security staff who oversaw the many after-hours time and the Reference Room staff—Bev Paty, Chantaal Ryane, Judy Root, Marion Tustanoff, Diane Wardle, and Carolyn Webber—who helped me locate material and manage the 'blinkety blank' microfiche machines. Also thanks to Kelly-Ann Turkington for arranging images from the B.C. Archives. At the University of Victoria Legacy Art Gallery (with the Maltwood Collection), who were in the middle of relocating, I thank Carolyn Riedel, Joy Davis, and Cindy Vance. At the beginning of the research, the cooperation of Kym Hill and Kimberly Bryant of the Mercurio Gallery set me up for a good start. Gunter Heinrich at the Winchester Galleries also gave me some guidance. At St. Margaret's School Archivist Christine Godfrey helped me puzzle out Ina Uhthoff's involvement there, and Stuart Brambley at Glenlyon-Norfolk School provided relevant information. The City of Victoria Archives' Sarah

Rathjen helped me trace photographs and other material. Thanks to Bob MacIntyre, (Preparator/ Exhibition Coordinator Burnaby Art Gallery) for first suggesting to Mona that Ina Uhthoff would be a good candidate for the UABC series.

Thank you also goes to the people who shared their art work, stories, research, and expertise: Alberta Culture and Community Spirit (Sheelagh Dunlap), Robert Amos, Archives Association of B.C., B.C. Museums Association (Jim Harding), Rosemary James Cross, David Emery, Esquimalt Archives (Sherri Robinson), Betty Gordon Funke, National Gallery of Canada (Charles Hill), Glasgow School of Art (Susannah Waters), Leslie Glazier, Glenbow Museum (Colleen Sharpe), Sylvia Graham, Canadian Heritage Information Network (Sylvie Roy), Geri Hinton, Peter Hinton and Lyn Kelly, Vincent Holmes, Sue Horton (née Docia Jones), Judith Kay, Barb Latham, David Marryatt, David Martin (Martin-Zambito Fine Art), Pat Martin Bates, Kathleen Metcalf, Michael Morris, Roberta Pazdro, Hannah Reinhart, Seattle Art Museum (Ann Nolte, Cindy Wilson, Sarah Berman), Gary Sim (B.C. Artists Research), Kirsten Skov, Thisbe Stewart (née Fletcher), Maria Tippett, Nicholas Tuele (former Art Gallery of Greater Victoria Curator), Victoria Genealogy Society (Leila Muldrew), Victoria Sketch Club (John Lover), and Gerry and Marianne Webb.

A most important thank you goes to publisher Mona Fertig for enhancing my retirement years by enticing me into researching and writing for the *Unheralded Artists of British Columbia* series and then encouraging and guiding me along the way. A huge thank-you goes to my husband, Bob Dean, who kept my computer in top form and the house chores managed so that I could devote time to the project. I thank Pat Winram, my tech savy friend, who cooled my temper and enlightened me with the non-intuitive aspects of Word, especially with the new computer given to me mid-project by my husband. Thank you to those careful and conscientious editors and readers: Claudia Cornwall and Judith Brand. Thanks to the superior work of photographer Janet Dwyer, book designer Jan Westendorp, indexer Sheilagh Simpson. Lastly, thanks go to my daughters Heather and Susan, my sister Nelia, and many friends, who encouraged my writing, while making sure that I got some breaks to enjoy other parts of my life.

ENDNOTES

INTRODUCTION

1   Edythe Hembroff-Schleicher, *Emily Carr: The Untold Story*, Saanichton, BC: Hancock House Publishers, 1978

CHAPTER ONE: SCOTTISH START

1   Statutory Births 510/010144, Scotland
2   Muriel Thom (née Uhthoff), handwritten memory of her family in Nancy White Collection of personal papers pertaining to her grandmother Ina D.D. Uhthoff. Muriel included research on the name "Jemima", citing Jemima Campbell, who married Philip Yorke, the 2ⁿᵈ Earl of Hardwicke. The family chose the name, but they were not direct descendants.
3   Ibid.
4   Ibid. B.C. Archives, T 4134:1, Roberta Pazdro interview with John C. Uhthoff, April 11, 1984
5   B.C. Archives
6   Susannah Waters, Archivist, Glasgow School of Art (GSA), correspondence, May 17, 2011, regarding school records; Nancy White Collection
7   Waters; David Forrester Wilson (1905–1906, 1906–1907), William Edward Frank Britten (1911–1912), Paul Artot (1907–1908, 1910–1911, 1911–1912) and Maurice Greiffenhagen (1910–1911, 1912–1913)
8   Ina Uhthoff, correspondence to Colin Graham of her memories of art in Victoria, undated, AGGV, 1972 Exhibition File
9   A.R.E. refers to being an associate of what became the Royal Society of Etchers and Engravers, Susannah Waters, email to author, December, 2011
10   "New Art School Is Opened in Victoria," news clipping in Uhthoff Family collection, circa 1926. GSA records do not show these teachers, so it is unclear when she studied with these artists. She possibly took courses other than those at the GSA 1906–1913, while studying to be a teacher or teaching prior to marriage 1914–1919
11   "Scotswoman's Success in Canada," news clipping in Uhthoff Family Collection, no date or newspaper cited
12   Gary Sim, *Art and Artists in Exhibition: Vancouver 1890–1950*, BC Artists-Sim Research\BC Artists-Sim Research, Release 2.03
13   Nancy White Collection of Ina D.D. Uhthoff art

CHAPTER TWO: WESTERN CANADA ADVENTURE

1   Notes entitled "Post Graduation Trip to British Columbia" revised to "A Trip to the Canadian Wild West," p. 3, Nancy White Collection
2   Ibid. The Frasers' son, Bill came to Ledlanet Farm as a teenager in 1912, according to Harrison Memorial Church history, cretonbc.com/anglican/harrison.htm
3   Ibid.
4   Ibid. A photograph shows a group of unidentified men and women, probably at Crawford Bay.
5   Ibid. The drawings *Thoroughfare* and *An Oldtimer* derive from this period, news clipping hand-dated 1917, "Canadian Pictures," tells of Ina Campbell's solo exhibition of her Canadian work at the Ralph Proud Gallery on Gordon Street.
6   Maria Tippett and Douglas Cole, *From Desolation to Splendour*, Vancouver: Clarke, Irwin & Co., 1977, p. 124
7   "Service Held," February 25, 1971, Death Registration for E.J. Uhthoff, 1971–09–003333, B.C. Archives, PDP File; also Uhthoff Family Tree, Uhthoff Family Papers
8   Muriel Thom, in Nancy White Collection
9   B.C. Archives, Uhthoff Painting, Prints, and Drawings File, "Mrs. Uhthoff Dies Suddenly," obituary 1971
10   "Service Held," The involvement of E.J. Uhthoff's company in the war is described in an article about the battalion's reunion, "Old Boys of the 54ᵗʰ Kootenay Battalion Held Reunion," November 18, 1937, probably the Nelson newspaper. A certificate signed by the Governor General of Canada acknowledges his service as a lieutenant, dated May 1, 1919, Michael Uhthoff Collection
11   *London Gazette*, issue 30424, December 12, 1917, 54ᵗʰ Kootenay Batallion Honours and Award U Index, http://members.shaw.ca/cef54/indu.htm
12   Ibid. *Trench Mats*, Uhthoff Family Collection. Ted was not the only person with drawing skill in the Uhthoff line; Nancy White Collection has a careful pencil drawing of a rural scene with cottage, trees and arched stone bridge over a creek, dated 1858 and signed L. Uhthoff (probably Ted's father, Ludolfo Uhthoff).

CHAPTER THREE: TEACHING AND
MARRIAGE IN SCOTLAND

1 Correspondence from the Scotch Education
   Department, July 1, 1916, and with
   Superannuation #37.999 as of September, 1916;
   Glasgow Provincial Committee for the Training
   of Teachers, October 4, 1916, Nancy White
   Collection

2 Nancy White Collection

3 Ibid., letter dated May 3, 1924

4 Ibid., letter dated April 30, 1924

5 B.C. Archives, T 4134:1, Pazdro interview;
   correspondence from Michael Uhthoff,
   January 12, 2011

6 Ina Uhthoff, correspondence to Colin Graham of
   her memories of her past and art in Victoria, no
   date, AGGV, 1972 Exhibition File

7 Ibid.

8 Ibid.

9 Ibid.

10 Ibid.

11 Sim, Art and Artists in Exhibition, chapter 1,
   note 12

12 News clipping, hand-dated 1917, "Canadian
   Pictures" solo exhibition at the [Ralph] Proud
   Gallery; Nancy White Collection

13 Royal Society for the Encouragement of Arts,
   Manufacturers, and Commerce, London,
   England, Society's House, Adelphi, London.
   Since her married name is on the certificate, the
   date must be no earlier than 1919.

14 Nancy White Collection of art

15 Nancy White Collection of photos

CHAPTER FOUR: KOOTENAYS TO THE
CAPITAL: THE VICTORIA SCHOOL OF
ART YEARS

1 Uhthoff, correspondence to Colin Graham,
   chapter 3, note 6

2 Notes on Life in Crawford Bay, 1919–1938,
   Michael Uhthoff collection of papers

3 Uhthoff Family History, Nancy White
   Collection. A family photograph shows Ina as a
   young mother with John.

4 Wrigley and Wrigley-Henderson B.C. Directories
   list E.J. Uhthoff in Crawford Bay but on "active
   service" in 1919. He is listed in 1920, 1921
   and 1922 though no employment is indicated.
   There are no listings for the Uhthoffs in either
   Crawford Bay or Victoria in 1923, 1924 and
   1925. Notes on Life in Crawford Bay, 1919–1938,

   Michael Uhthoff Collection of papers

5 Nancy White Collection

6 Uhthoff, correspondence to Colin Graham, May
   17, 1927, Victoria Daily Colonist, Michael Uhthoff
   Collection

7 See chapter 3, notes 3 and 4

8 S.M. Carter, ed., Who's Who in British Columbia,
   Victoria: Admark, 1931, pp. 106–107

9 B.C. Archives, T 4134:1, Pazdro interview

10 Joy Uhthoff, interview with author, January 23,
   2011

11 "Art Exhibition by Mrs. Uhthoff's Pupils to
   Last Fortnight," news clipping in Uhthoff
   Family Collection, 1926, no newspaper cited. It
   indicated that the exhibit was the work of Ina's
   students from the past year

12 Patrick Dunae, The School Record: A Guide to
   Government Archives Relating to Public Education
   in BC 1852–1946, Victoria: B.C. Archives &
   Records Service, 1992

13 Uhthoff, correspondence to Colin Graham

14 Anthony W. Rogers, W.P. Weston, Educator and
   Artist: The Development of the British Ideas in
   the Art Curriculum of B.C. Public Schools, PhD
   dissertation, UBC, Vancouver. Weston had come
   to B.C. in 1909 and taught at the Provincial
   Normal School from 1914–1946. With his British
   educational training and ideas, he was largely
   responsible for the official art text in 1924,
   completely responsible for its 1933 revision and
   instrumental in the 1936 rewriting of all art
   programmes. One of the first artists to develop a
   new vision of the western Canadian landscape,
   he received national recognition by becoming
   a charter member of the Canadian Group of
   Painters in 1933 and the first B.C. Associate of
   the Royal Canadian Academy in 1936.

15 Uhthoff, correspondence to Colin Graham.
   She noted that he brought in Jock (J.W.G.)
   MacDonald (from Edinburgh), the Sundoor
   Fabric Designer to head the Design Department.
   Also Charles H. Scott, "A Short Art History
   of British Columbia" from Behind the Palette
   Vancouver: Vancouver School of Art, c.
   1916–1947, pp. 4–6 [reference located in, W.W.
   Thom, The Fine Arts in Vancouver 1880–1930: An
   Historical Survey, MA thesis, UBC 1969] Also on
   staff were Grace Melvin (also Glasgow School
   of Art), F.H. Varley, Charles Marega and Kate
   Smith Hoole

16 Scott, A Short Art History of British Columbia

17   "Lieutenant Governor Officiates at Opening of Arts and Crafts Display," *Victoria Daily Colonist*, October 21, 1925

18   Ina D.D. Uhthoff, "Art Pioneer Fine Painter," *Victoria Daily Colonist*, circa 1950s. He had won the Keith Prize in 1903 for the best work by a student in the life classes.

19   Margaret Kitto was an established, respected artist and teacher. Also "Art Exhibition by Mrs. Uhthoff's Pupils to Last Fortnight," news clipping in Uhthoff Family Collection, dated 1926 and identifying the exhibit open from April 15 to May 1, indicates Ina as a newcomer, who had been teaching for "a little more than a year" in Victoria.

20   "New Art School Is Opened in Victoria," news clipping in Uhthoff Family Collection, no date or newspaper cited

21   Roberta Pazdro, *B.C. Women Artists, 1885–1985*, Victoria: AGGV, 1985, p. 14. Also Sim, *Art and Artists in Exhibition*, chapter 1, note 12. One student cited was Patience Birley.

22   B.C. Archives, T 4134:1, Pazdro, interview; correspondence from Michael Uhthoff, January 12, 2011. He also remembered that she was the sole support for the family.

23   "Art Exhibition by Mrs. Uhthoff's Pupils to Last Fortnight," news clipping, Uhthoff Family Collection, 1926, no newspaper cited

24   "Art School Exhibition Shows Promising Work: Talent of Unusual Character Discovered in Display of Work by Students of Mrs. Uhthoff—Thorough Knowledge Shown by Instructor," May 17, 1927, *Victoria Daily Colonist*

25   Ibid. The work of Margaret Izard, P. Fairbairn and Angela Davis were mentioned among the more skilled drawings.

26   Ibid. Other students mentioned were Daphne Gillespie, Ev Fordyce, Evangeline Pease, Helen Streatfeild, Peggy Hodgins, Cynthia Clayton and Amy Adamson.

27   Ibid. "Scotswoman's Success in Canada," news clipping in Uhthoff Family Collection, no date or newspaper cited

28   Ibid. Under Drawing and Painting, the following options were listed: figure drawing and portrait painting in all mediums, construction and anatomy of the human figure, action study and memory drawing, study of the antique, pictorial composition, book illustration, mural and interior decoration, posters and magazine drawings in pen and ink and process black and white, decorative pen drawing for reproduction. Under Design and Applied Art, there was nature drawing in pencil, chalks, watercolours, and pen and ink; application to designs for reproduction, advertising and commercial purposes, stenciling, embroidery, pottery, wood-staining, gesso, block printing and book plates. Other subjects included lettering, inscriptions, illuminating, landscape sketching, etching and monotypes on zinc and copper, including the process of grounding the plates, biting in the acids and printing; silversmithing, including the making of jewelry, etching of semi-precious stones, chain making; and animal drawing at Beacon Hill Park.

29   "Victoria School of Art," *Farm, Orchard, and Green*, July, 1927, news clipping in Uhthoff Family Collection, "Mrs. Uhthoff believes in methods that will bring out the individuality of each student… they are encouraged towards more distinctive effort."

30   Ibid.

31   Ibid.

32   "Island Arts Exhibition of High Standard," *Victoria Daily Times*, October 21, 1931, p. 6

33   Catalogue for the Nineteenth Annual Exhibition of Original Paintings, Drawings, Designs, and Crafts, IACS, October 23–31, 1928, B.C. Archives, NWp707.4I82a

34   John Lover, *The Victoria Sketch Club: A Centennial Celebration*, Victoria: Printorium Bookworks, 2008, p. 14

35   Carter, S.E., *Who's Who in B.C.* Victoria Admark 1931, p. 106–107

36   Sue Horton, interview with author, October 23, 2011

37   St Margaret's School Magazine/Cardinal (yearbook) 1926, 1927 and the St. Margaret's School Prospectus, 1928, St. Margaret's School Archives, 1080 Lucas Avenue, Victoria, Christine Godfrey, Archivist

38   B.C. Archives, T 4134:1, Pazdro, interview

39   Sue Horton interview. Sue remembered taking some of her art classes and thought of Ina as a hard worker and a gifted artist. Though with her accent Ina might pronounce some words differently, causing some girls to laugh, Sue remembered her as a good teacher, who would teach classes in exchange for Muriel's tuition.

40   Uhthoff, correspondence to Colin Graham

41   Ibid.

42 "Ina D.D. Uhthoff," *Artists in Canada: A Dictionary of Canadian Artists,* Canadian Heritage Information Network, National Gallery of Canada, pro.rcip-chin.gc.ca, reports that she taught in the school until 1932. However, Ina is in the photograph for the "Staff of Teachers' Summer School Here," *Victoria Daily Colonist,* August 2, 1934. The poster flyer for the Victoria School of Art lists her as a "Lecturer at Provincial Summer School for Teachers," Michael Uhthoff

43 B.C. Archives, T 4134:1, Pazdro interview

44 Patrick Dunae, *The School Record,* p. 55. More information about John Kyle: "John Kyle Funeral Set for Tuesday," March 3, 1958, *Victoria Daily Times* and "Artist, Educator John Kyle Dies," March 30, 1958, *Victoria Daily Colonist,* AGGV Archives Scrapbook. He was a native of Hawick, Scotland, studied at the Royal College of Art (receiving a prize for Anatomy), came to B.C. in 1905 as Supervisor of Drawing in Vancouver Schools as well as Director of Night School Classes. He died in 1958 at age 87.

45 Uhthoff, correspondence to Colin Graham

46 Ibid. It is not clear whether she is referring solely to her taking over the Kingston Street School of Pottery and integrating it with Victoria School of Art or whether he gave her assistance in the mid-1920s when she was first establishing her school.

47 Information Form, National Gallery of Canada, Ottawa, completed by Ina D.D. Uhthoff, and received August 23, 1965 by the NGC Library; also Dunae, *The School Record,* p. 73

48 The author, Nancy de Bertrand Lugrin, is later referred to as Nancy de Bertrand Lugrin Shaw or Mrs. Shaw.

49 Other sketches showed Captain Vancouver at Nootka, Alexander McKenzie in Bella Coola, a trapper with his dogs, the tent store for the gold rush miners on the Leech River, the Old Cariboo Road and Placer mining in the Interior as well as a First Nation canoe and teepee.

50 "Book Tea Is Big Function: Four Hundred Women's Canadian Club Members at Launching of Volume Yesterday at Empress," November, 1928, *Victoria Daily Colonist*

51 Ibid. Ina was introduced with the foreman printer, Isaac Dixon; she thanked Annie Bullen (Mrs. Fitzherbert-Bullen) of the Club as well as Miss Cree and Alma Russell from the Provincial Library.

52 Colin Graham, *Ina D.D.Uhthoff: Memorial Exhibition,* Victoria: AGGV, 1972. He also wrote that they sponsored another class during the next year.

53 Mark Tobey, en.wikipedia. org/wiki/Mark_Tobey

54 Edythe Hembroff-Schleicher, *Emily Carr: The Untold Story,* Saanichton, BC: Hancock House Publishers, 1978, p. 224

55 Ibid., p. 230. Napier was Provincial Assistant Public Works Engineer and Department Manager of Railways

56 Ibid., pp. 229–230

57 Tippett and Cole, *From Desolation to Splendour,* pp. 97, 124–125; Lover, *The Victoria Sketch Club,* p. 14

58 Sim, *Art and Artists in Exhibition,* chapter 1, note 12

59 Charlie Hill, Curator, National Gallery of Canada, Email to author January, 2011; Sim, *Art and Artists in Exhibition*

60 Canadian National Exhibition Catalogue, 1930, Vancouver Art Gallery Archives, email from Cheryl Seigel, Librarian, January, 2012. *The Life and Art of Mildred Valley Thornton* by Sheryl Salloum was published in June 2011, the 4th in the *Unheralded Artists of BC* series by Mother Tongue Publishing

61 Wrigley's B.C. Directory. Ina's 1929 residence was at 2408 San Carlos, while her art school was at 739 Yates St. E.J. (Ted) Uhthoff was not listed in the Directories for Victoria, Sardis or Crawford Bay, but in 1934 he had returned to Crawford Bay as a rancher. Also Notes by John C. Uhthoff, Michael Uhthoff Collection

62 In the Nancy White Collection of photos is Muriel at age 9 in her Monterey School division 7 class photo in 1931. In John Campbell Uhthoff's notes, he indicates that he attended Duncan Grammer School (just north of Victoria) in January 1929, studying with R.E. Honor. Why John was away for school is not explained – was he difficult or did going away from home for school reflect his parents' preferences with their British background? Michael Uhthoff Collection

63 Geri Hinton, wife of John's friend, Peter Hinton, interview with author, January 24, 2011 at her home in Saanich. She remembered that her husband had a long-time friendship with John Uhthoff and his wife Joy, extending from the boys' days at Monterey School. The Hintons

continue to have a number of works by Ina Uhthoff, so they were clearly supportive patrons of her work.

64 Sue Horton interview with author, October 23, 2011

65 Thisbe Stewart interview with author, January 6, 2012. The shortbread recipe that came from Ina to her daughter Muriel Thom, and then to grand-daughter Nancy Thom White was published in Nancy's former husband's cookbook, *The Summer Shack Cookbook* by Jasper White.

66 Nancy White Collection

67 B.C. Archives, T 4134:1, Pazdro, interview

68 Thom, Nancy White Collection. Perhaps her sister Edie helped her financially with the trip; later Edie wrote that since she had no children, her estate would go to Ina.

69 Notes on Crawford Bay, Michael Uhthoff Collection, 1919–1938. John carefully sketched the lamp, noting the lifestyle. While Ted worked at W.O. Burden's camp, he was one of nine men who fell from a truck transporting them, putting him in the Kaslo Hospital with an injured knee in October-November, 1931.

70 S.M. Carter, ed., *Who's Who in British Columbia*, Victoria: Admark Limited, 1931, pp. 106–107

71 Keith Walker, *Truth and Courage: An Informal History of Glenlyon School 1932–1986*, Victoria: Glenlyon-Norfolk School, 2006, p. 44. A photo of Ina at that time is included beside the text. Also Uhthoff, Ina Correspondence to Colin Graham, Feb. 8, 1970 AGGV 1971 Exhibition File

72 Edythe Hembroff-Schleicher, *The Modern Room*, Victoria: B.C. Provincial Archives, 1981, p. 12

73 Ibid. When recreating the exhibit, Edythe was unable to locate the original *Cedars,* so she used a charcoal drawing, which she remembered being similar. It was owned by Ina's son John Uhthoff and was easily obtained for the exhibit.

74 Ibid. In addition to the *Cedars* in the Modern Room, Ina exhibited watercolours *Rocks and Ice Plants, The Biltmore Beach, The Court House, A Kootenay Creek* and oil *Kokanee Glacier* in the traditional section. All painted in Santa Barbara.

75 Catalogue, 23rd Annual Exhibition of Paintings, Drawings, Designs and Crafts, IACS, October 11–22, 1932, NWp707.4I82a

76 Hembroff-Schleicher, *The Modern Room,* p. 12. The text was changed because Ina's son John had not felt comfortable with her view. Correspondence from Jerry Mossop, Head of

Paintings, Prints, and Drawings, Provincial Archives of British Columbia, June 23, 1981, Michael Uhthoff Collection

77 Tippett and Cole, *From Desolation to Splendour*, p. 124

78 Hembroff-Schleicher, *The Modern Room,* pp. 12–13

79 Hembroff-Schleicher, *Emily Carr,* p. 352

80 Hembroff-Schleicher, *The Modern Room,* p. 12. Clive Bell, who was married to Virginia Woolf's sister Vanessa, was associated with the Bloomsbury Group and formalism (Thus he wrote, "to appreciate a work of art we need bring with us nothing from life, no knowledge of its ideas and affairs, no familiarity with emotions."), en.wikipedia.org/ wkik/Clive_Bell

81 Thom, Nancy White collection

82 Emily Carr, *Hundreds and Thousands: A Journal of an Artist,* Toronto: Irwin, 1996, p. 172; passage identified as describing Ina Uhthoff: Hembroff-Schleicher, *Emily Carr: The Untold Story,* p. 229

83 B.C. Archives, T 4134:1, Pazdro interview

84 Audrey St. Denys Johnson, *Arts Beat: The Arts in Victoria,* Winnipeg: J. Gordon Shillingford/ Hignell Printing, 1994, p. 15

85 Ibid.

86 Ibid., pp. 182–183. While at home, Audrey found a hand-printing press in a rear garden studio with a north-facing window. She occupied herself with lino and woodblock prints and making Christmas cards for her mother. Audrey was not able to pursue her art studies further due helping nurse her father in failing health.

87 "Permanent Gallery Will Be Sought by Arts Group of City," *Victoria Daily Colonist,* November 5, 1935

88 Information Form, National Gallery of Canada,

89 Thom, Nancy White Collection, Blue Binder. She also observed that Victoria was far from the mainstream, and there was no Canadian equivalent of the w.p.a. [Works Progress Administration which employed artists and craftsman during the depression in the U.S.]

90 Sim, *Art and Artists in Exhibition*, chapter 1, note 12

91 B.C. Archives, T 4134:1, Pazdro, interview

92 Ibid.; Thom, Nancy White Collection. John also recalled that his mother remembered seeing her father after he died, lying on the couch. She called the rest of the family, but by the time they came into the room, he was not there. He

mentioned how serious she was about seeing ghosts of the deceased.

93 "Win High Lifesaving Honors," October 5, 1935, no newspaper cited, Michael Uhthoff Collection

94 Ibid. Michael Uhthoff Collection

95 Nancy White collection, news clipping, "Group Wins Junior Championship," *Victoria Daily Colonist,* May 5, 1935, Muriel starred as "Franchette from France."

96 Ina's painting of Mt. Baker was originally purchased at her Memorial Exhibition by Colin Graham for his personal collection. Sue Horton interview with author, October 23, 2011

97 B.C. Archives, T 4134:1, Pazdro, interview

98 Ina Uhthoff, correspondence to Colin Graham

99 B.C. and Yukon Directory, 1938–1944; in 1943, Ina and Muriel lived at 2–1385 Manor Road, where Ina had lived and had a studio in 1927 and 1928. She listed herself as an Instructor for the Dominion Provincial Youth Training Centre in 1938 and 1939.

100 Colin Graham, *Ina D.D. Uhthoff: Memorial Exhibition,* AGGV, 1972

101 B.C. Archives, T 4134:1, Pazdro, interview

102 Uhthoff, correspondence to Colin Graham

103 Ibid.

104 Ibid.

105 Roberta Pazdro, in Nicholas Tuele, Christina Johnson-Dean and Roberta Pazdro, *B.C. Women Artists 1885–1985,* Victoria: AGGV, 1985, p. 14

106 Rosemary Alicia Brown, *Katherine Emma Maltwood: Artist 1878–1961,* Victoria: University of Victoria, Maltwood Museum and Gallery, Sono Nis Press, 1981, p. 54

107 Betty Gordon Funke, *Tweed Curtain Pioneers,* Victoria: Trafford Publishing 2006, p. 17

108 "Adult Education," Miss J.E.M Bruce, with photographs, 1939, *Victoria Daily Colonist,* Magazine Features

109 Ibid.

110 B.C. Archives, B.C. Dept. of Education Annual Reports 1935–1943, D31 Reel 9, p. B84. The Victoria School of Art offered full-time and part-time courses in Drawing and Painting from Life, Plant Form and Design, Commercial Art, Lettering and Illuminating, Historical Costume and Dress Design, Lino-block Printing, Colour, Composition, and Illustration, Modelling, Pottery and Crafts.

111 "Arts and Crafts Exhibit Opened," *Victoria Daily Times,* April 9, 1940, p. 5

112 Rosemary Cross, "Interview with Christina Johnson-Dean," February 4, 2011, at Cross's home on Linden Avenue. Lilian Emerson later married and took the surname Rogers.

113 Ibid.

114 Funke, Tweed Curtain Pioneers, p. 15. The sketch is dated 1946, so it may have been looking back on their lessons. Mr. Braur was probably the model for the painting entitled "Canadian" in the Michael Uhthoff collection.

115 Ibid., p. 16

116 Ibid.

117 Ibid.

118 Ibid. Lilian was grateful to her teacher. Ina had been the one to encourage her to submit two large oils to the Vancouver Jury Show. They hung next to Lawren Harris's work; Canada Packers bought them both.

119 Ibid.

120 Robert Amos, "Ewan's CV Shines a Spotlight on City's Developing Art Scene," September 19, 1987, *Victoria Times Colonist,* in Michael Uhthoff collection

121 B.C. Archives, B.C. Dept. of Education Annual Reports 1935–1943, D31 Reel 9, p. D93

122 History of Victoria's Harbour , http://www.victoriaharbour.org/h history.php, April 22, 2012

123 B.C. Archives, B.C. Dept. of Education Annual Reports 1935–1943, D31 Reel 9, p. B71

124 Marion Brymner Appleton, ed, *Who's Who in Northwest Art: A Directory of Persons in the Pacific Northwest Working in the Media of Painting, Sculpture, Graphic Arts, and Handicrafts,* Seattle: Frank McCaffrey, 1941, p. 70

125 B.C. and Yukon Directory, 1943; Sue Horton, interview with author, October 23, 2011

126 Joy Uhthoff interview with author, January 23, 2011, at her home in Qualicum Beach. John had apparently disappointed his mother when he joined the Air Force, rather than continuing at UBC. Ina said, "He threw it in my face," but like so many parents, she came to accept his decision, and they remained close. John graduated as a fighter pilot on December 3, 1942. "Flyer Leaves After Furlough Here," news clipping, Nancy White collection, no newspaper cited, dated 1942. John spent some time in Victoria before heading east.

127 B.C. Archives, T 4134:1, Pazdro, interview. The

painting of the fishing gear is currently in the collection of Michael Uhthoff.

128 Lorne Render, *Mountains and Sky,* Calgary: Glenbow-Alberta Institute, McClelland and Stewart West, 1974, p. 101. Ina's paintings were purchased by the Glenbow Foundation in early 1961 when Moncrieff Williamson was Director for the Art Department. He had formerly been with the AGGV (in charge of extensions to bring exhibits to places outside Victoria) and knew the value of her work. Correspondence from Moncrieff Williamson to Ina D.D. Uhthoff, November 29, 1960 and May 17, 1971, Michael Uhthoff Collection

129 "Arts and Crafts Display Attractive," *Victoria Times Colonist*, October 29, 1943; "Pottery Features Crafts Exhibition," *Victoria Daily Times*, October 25, 1943; "Arts and Crafts Display Varied and Distinctive," *Victoria Daily Colonist*, October 24, 1943

130 *Self Portrait,* 1942, owned by a private collector

131 Marguerite Hobbs, handwritten note in Artist's File, AGGV

CHAPTER FIVE: ARTIST, GALLERY FOUNDER AND COLUMNIST

1 SculptSite.com, Peggy Walton Packard Sculpture; Betty Gordon Funke, *Tweed Curtain Pioneers,* Victoria: Trafford, 2006, p. 18

2 Funke, *Tweed Curtain Pioneers,* p. 18

3 Kathleen Metcalf, interview with author by email and phone, January, 2012

4 Ann Nolte interview with author by phone, January 2012. She also remembered Ann Kipling, a well-known B.C. artist, who often drew horses in Ina's studio. Later in life Ann Nolte returned to Victoria and worked for Capital Regional Health, where she met another unheralded artist, Edythe Hembroff-Schleicher, who continued to paint as an elderly woman.

5 "Victoria Artist's Exhibit to Aid Red Cross," August 27, 1944, *Victoria Daily Colonist,* news clipping in Uhthoff Family Collection

6 One of the *Woman Welder* [or *Girl Welder at Work*] paintings is currently located at the AGGV (#1993.050.001) John C. Uhthoff as a pilot is in the Michael Uhthoff Collection. She was proud of John's service, but there were certainly worries, especially when a letter home casually mentioned that his plane had been hit in a post-invasion operation. With Our Servicemen,"

news clipping in Nancy White Collection; no date, no newspaper cited, but Ina was living at 468 Beach Drive

7 "Victoria Artist's Exhibit to Aid Red Cross," August 27, 1944, *Victoria Daily Colonist*

8 Ibid.

9 Ibid. Many of the paintings are untitled and show workers, boats, machinery, gas tanks, spools etc. They are in the collections of the B.C. Archives and David Emery. B.C. Archives Paintings, Prints, and Drawings File, excerpt from 150th Celebration Companion Book with photocopy of her painting of workers leaving the factory.

10 Ibid.

11 There are several *Woman Welder* [or *Girl Welder at Work*] paintings. The painting sent to Odessa has not been located. David Emery, art collector and boilermaker, believes that the painting depicts the Bay St. boiler plant, due to the shapes in the background.

12 Charles H. Scott, "A Short Art History of British Columbia," *Behind the Palette,* Vancouver: Vancouver School of Art, c. 1946–1947, pp. 4–6 [reference located in W.W. Thom, *The Fine Arts in Vancouver 1880–1930: An Historical Survey,* unpublished MA thesis, UBC, 1969]

13 Ibid.

14 "To Odessa, Port of Five Harbors… Go Paintings of B.C.'s Industrial Life," January 20, 1945, *Vancouver Daily Province,* p. 3. Other artists included W.J.B. Newcombe, Viola Campbell, J. Delisle Parker, Gilbert H. Kershaw, Aylmer Pratt, John Roberts and Platon V. Ustinov.

15 David Marryatt, interview by phone with author, January 18, 2011

16 Joy Uhthoff, interview with author. "He was looking quite smart in his military uniform, and she recalled that "I didn't look too bad myself." Joy had a bouffant hairdo and guessed that John was not sure of his dancing skills, so he said to her, "If you didn't wear your hair so damn high, I might be able to see where I'm going."

17 Joy Uhthoff, interview with author. They took a train to London, where they stayed in a hotel, which was "frightful." Joy's mother had been so helpful, and now she was on her own, though some other war brides helped her with her son, who was not yet walking. Joy recalled being "herded" on the trip, though there was certainly enough to eat on the ship, the *Letitia,* which took

them to Halifax, before the train across Canada to Vancouver.

18 Ibid.

19 Ibid.

20 "17 Local Girls in Final St. John Overseas Group," September 20, 1945, no newspaper cited; "Will Help With Drive in Districts: Leaves for England," September 8, 1945, no newspaper cited, News clippings, Uhthoff Family Collection

21 Nancy White Collection of personal papers, Blue Binder. 1946–1949

22 Ibid., correspondence, Muriel Uhthoff to Ina Uhthoff, December 4, 1946; August 7, 1946

23 Joy Uhthoff, interview with author

24 Victoria City and Vancouver Island Directories, 1944–1971. Only the directories for 1965–1969 lists "instructor B.C. Government" in addition to her occupation as an artist.

25 Colin Graham, *Ina D.D. Uhthoff: Memorial Exhibition*, Victoria: Art Gallery of Greater Victoria, 1972

26 Her studios were located as follows: 1944–1946 at 918 Government Street, 1947–1948 at 534 Broughton Street, 1949–1952 at 1221 Wharf Street. Once the AGGV was established, Ina's studio appears to have been in her home, and she taught at the gallery.

27 Robert Amos, "History of Today's Artists Is Still in the Creation Process," June 22, 1996, *Victoria Times Colonist*. A reader indicated the location, Victoria City Archives, General Artists Clippings File

28 Sim, *Art and Artists in Exhibition; Information Form*, National Gallery of Canada, completed by Ina Uhthoff, Aug. 23, 1965. She showed *Dutch Canadian* and *Forest Piece* in the 16th Annual Exhibition in 1947, and *Blue Mood* and *Still Life with Oranges* in the 19th Annual Exhibition in 1950.

29 Thom, "The Fine Arts in Vancouver 1880–1930

30 Mary Jo Hughes, *Vision Into Reality*, Victoria: AGGV, 2009, p. 15–16

31 Rosemary Alicia Brown, *Katherine Emma Maltwood*, p. 54

32 "History of the Collection," Maltwood Collection, University of Victoria, maltwood. uvic.ca/k_maltwood/history/slangdale.html

33 The Hon. Mark Hudson Kearley, born March 3, 1895, to Hudson Ewbanke Kearley, 1st Viscount Devonport and Selina Chester, educated at Eton College and Oxford University (Magdalene College). He had been a Prisoner of War in Germany during World War I. http://thepeerage.com/p36949.htm

34 List of Initial Committee for the Victoria Branch of the Canadian Federation of Artists in 1944 and Lists of Board of Directors, AGGV, Archives. In October 1944, the Honourable Mark Kearley was listed as Chairman, and Ina Uthoff was Vice Chairman. Isabel Hobbs was Secretary, and C.J. Turpin, Will Menelaws and H.G. Parker were members. By December, others had joined, including Stewart Clark, who served as Treasurer.

35 Yvonne H. Stevenson, "Letter to the Editor: Art Gallery Founders," November 26, 1957, *Victoria Daily Times*, AGGV, Archives Scrapbook. She had been Executive Secretary from September 1946 to September 1947 for the Arts Centre of Greater Victoria.

36 "Opening by the Governor General Viscount Alexander of the Little Gallery at Thomas Plimley's auto showroom at 965 Yates St.," July 19, 1946, Johnson's Arts Beat, *Victoria Daily Colonist*. The Little Centre was sometimes called the Little Gallery. Photographs show the building and opening; Hughes, Vision to Reality, pp. 17–18

37 Hughes, *Vision Into Reality*, pp. 17–18

38 Joy Uhthoff, interview with author

39 Stevenson, "Letter to the Editor: Art Gallery Founders"

40 Funke, *Tweed Curtain Pioneers*, p. 18

41 "Island Arts and Crafts Show at Little Centre," *Victoria Daily Colonist*, February 25, 1947, p. 17

42 Greg Webb, interview with author, January 22, 2011 at his home in Brentwood Bay. Greg and his wife, Mary Ann, have an Ina Uhthoff painting, "Calla Lilies and Oriental Gown,"which was bought at Kathleen Agnew's Garden Party, when funds were being raised for the gallery.

43 Hughes, *Vision Into Reality*, p. 31, note 10

44 Johnson, *Arts Beat*, p. 187

45 B.C. Archives, Paintings, Prints, and Drawings File, "Talented Victorians," October 23, 1948, *Victoria Daily Times*. Others exhibitors were Unity Baile, Gertrude Snider, Peggy Walton Packard, Tony C.A. Law, Barbara Woodward and I. Eldridge.

46 "Uhthoff Art Exhibit Opened in City," December 8, 1948, *Victoria Daily Colonist*, Uhthoff Family Collection. It also announced the opening of

new premises at 823 Broughton Street in the Mellnor Building.

47 "Art Lovers Attend Outstanding Exhibit," December 17, 1948, *Victoria Times Colonist,* B.C. Archives, Paintings, Prints, and Drawings File

48 Colin Graham, *Ina D.D. Uhthoff: Memorial Exhibition,* Victoria: AGGV, 1972; Funke, *Tweed Curtain Pioneers,* p. 19. Yvonne Stevenson, the author of *Burns and His Bonnie Jean: The Romance of Robert Burns and Jean Armour,* was a direct descendant of the Armour family. She was a member of the Canadian Authors Association.

49 Hughes, *Vision Into Reality,* p. 18

50 Johnson, *Arts Beat,* p. 188

51 "Arts Centre of Greater Victoria," 1950–1951. Announcement of Forthcoming Exhibitions, AGGV Archives; "Art Centre Displays Striking Watercolors," no date or newspaper cited, positively reviews the work of Polk and Vitousek

52 Audrey St. D. Johnson, "Jury Show Brings Out Fine Pictures," November, 1950, *Victoria Daily Times*

53 "Arts Centre Buys Uhthoff Painting As Start of Permanent Collection," November, 1950, no newspaper cited; "Local Artist With Contribution," Friday, November 24, 1950, *Victoria Daily Times*; "Laying the Foundation," November 23, 1950, *Victoria Daily Times,* Uhthoff Family Collection. The list of works in the Jury Show does not include *Sunflowers,* so it may have been a later addition or *A Golden Glow* renamed.

54 Johnson, *Arts Beat,* p. 189

55 Letters from Muriel to Ina D.D. Uhthoff, December 15, 1947, Nancy White Collection

56 Ibid., letters dated June, 1947; August 7, 1946; September 15, 1947; July 12, 1948; September 13, 1948

57 Ibid., correspondence dated January 28, 1947. In March 1948, Muriel reported that her future father-in-law, Maurice Thom, wrote to Ina, probably to introduce himself and reassure her about their family. He mentioned that he had been in school with Ina's brother, Alec. Background on Trevor Thom: "Need Best Produce and Service," September 1975 news clipping, Nancy White Collection. Born in Naroibi, Kenya, where his father was a Commissionaire of Police in the British Colonial Service, Trevor was schooled in Scotland then joined the Royal Gurkha Rifle in 1939 and served in India.

58 Ibid., letter dated January 2, 1948

59 "Well-Known Victoria Girl Married in England," July 27, 1949, *Victoria Daily Colonist;* "Married in England," August 17, 1949, *Victoria Daily Colonist,* Uhthoff Family Collection. The first article identifies her as the daughter of Mr. and Mrs. E.J. Uhthoff, 401 Constance Avenue, continuing the official status of Ina as a married woman. Trevor was the son of Captain Maurice St. Clair Thom; his mother had recently passed away. Muriel and Trevor lived in Toronto after their marriage and had two daughters, Fiona Mary St. Clair (June 16, 1953) and Nancy Craigie St. Clair (August 31, 1954). They moved to Montreal, where Trevor worked for J.H. Ryder Machinery Corporation as a tire salesman. Nancy Thom White interview with author, October 23, 2011. On one memorable occasion, Muriel and her two daughters visited Victoria and went with Ina to Colin and Sylvia Graham's home. Sylvia had made chocolate éclairs, and her oldest son John taught the girls, clothed in "pretty little dresses," how to explode the éclairs by jumping on them. Sylvia Graham, interview with author. January 27, 2011

60 "Seven District Students UBC Graduates," *Nelson News,* June 14, 1949, Uhthoff Family Collection

61 "Prizes," *Vancouver Sun,* May 11, 1949, Uhthoff Family Collection

62 Hughes, *Vision Into Reality,* Victoria: AGGV, 2009, p. 18; note 19, p. 31; "Miss Sara Spencer Offers Family Residence to City as Art Gallery," *Victoria Daily Times,* July 21, 1951

63 Jim Nesbitt, "House Held Unsuitable for Priceless Paintings," no date, *Victoria Daily Colonist,* Uhthoff Family Collection

64 Hughes, *Vision Into Reality,* p. 18; note 17, p. 31. Hildegard Wyllie, born in London, England, was from the Richmond family, with several accomplished painters. She and her husband hosted many art circle events at their Saanich home, "Omeishan" (Sacred Mountain).

65 Ibid., p. 17

66 Ibid., p. 20

67 Graham, interview with author

68 Hughes, *Vision Into Reality,* p. 20; note 22, p. 31; correspondence Ina Uhthoff to Colin Graham, June 22, 1951, AGGV, Archives

69 Hughes, p. 20–21; note 25, p. 31; correspondence Colin Graham to Ina Uhthoff, July 13, 1951

70 Hughes, p. 21; note 26, p. 31; correspondence Colin Graham to Ina Uhthoff, August 5, 1951

71 Ibid.

72 Hughes, p. 18

73 Lists of Board of Directors, Art Gallery of Greater Victoria, Archives

74 Sylvia Graham, interview with author

75 Hughes, note 30, p. 31. The main exhibition spaces were named after people important to the founding: Spencer (after Sara Spencer), Kearley (after Mark Kearley) and Massey (after Vincent Massey).

76 Hughes, p. 22

77 "Modern Art at the Centre" and other Letters to the Editor, AGGV, Archives Scrapbooks. October, 1952

78 Ibid.

79 Mona Fertig, The Life and Art of George Fertig, Salt Spring Island: Mother Tongue, 2010, p. 84, note 10; p. 169, Minutes of Vancouver Art Gallery 27th Annual General Meeting, February 13, 1958

80 Colin Graham, "The Jury Show: Whys and Wherefores," October 18, 1952, Victoria Daily Times

81 Ibid.

82 Ken McAllister, "All Have Been Services," November 5, 1952, no newspaper cited, AGGV Archives Scrapbooks

83 Handwritten note beside news clippings, AGGV Archives Scrapbooks

84 Peter Loudon, "Pin-up Connoisseur Would Give Space to Impressionists," October 20, 1952, Victoria Daily Times, AGGV Archives Scrapbooks

85 Ibid.

86 Hughes, p. 23

87 Hughes, p. 25

88 "It's a Healthy Hobby: Doodling Businessmen to Get Chance at Art," November 3, 1952, Victoria Daily Times; "Converting the Doodlers," November 8, 1952, Victoria Daily Times, AGGV Archives Scrapbooks

89 Audrey St. D. Johnson,"Art's Good Companion Teaches New Classes," October 8, 1952, Victoria Daily Times, p. 25, AGGV Archives Scrapbooks

90 Funke, Tweed Curtain Pioneers, p. 88. Audrey had also attended St. Margaret's School.

91 David Marryatt, interview by phone with author, January 18, 2011

92 Ina D.D. Uhthoff, "Only Space for 80 Out of 226 Entries," April 9, 1957, Victoria Daily Colonist, AGGV Archives Scrapbooks

93 Michael Morris, email correspondence to author, January 2011

94 AGGV Archives, Scrapbooks, Lists, and Minutes

95 Ina D.D. Uhthoff, "Karsh Camera Portraits on Display," June 1, 1954, Victoria Daily Colonist, AGGV Archives Scrapbooks

96 Ina Uhthoff, "Spontaneous Child Art on Exhibit at Centre," January 6, 1954, Victoria Daily Colonist, AGGV Archives Scrapbooks

97 Ibid. "Children's Art on Display," January 6, 1954, shows some of the work displayed; Colin Graham also wrote about the children's exhibit: "Art in Review," January 16, 1954, Victoria Daily Times. He pushes readers to understand that though unconventional, children's art can exemplify a "fresh and stimulating fantasy." Also Ina D.D. Uhthoff, "Every Child a Genius Up to 10?" December 25, 1957, AGGV Archives Scrapbooks. In reviewing a student show at the gallery, Ina explained more about her thoughts about children's art: "The collection includes colorful and imaginative paintings, the most vigorous and spontaneous being the work of the six to nine year olds. When we got into the older groups, up to 16 years old, there is less promise shown. The child is adjusting himself to a more adult approach in which drawing plays an important part. The imagination is less active, the child wants to learn control."

98 Ina D.D. Uhthoff, "Water Color Exhibition Has Much to Offer," January 31, 1954, Victoria Daily Colonist, AGGV Archives Scrapbook

99 Ina D.D. Uhthoff, "Mexican Art Dominates Impressive Exhibition," May 5, 1957, Victoria Daily Colonist, AGGV Archives Scrapbook

100 Ina D.D. Uhthoff, "Masters on Display," February 14, 1956, Victoria Daily Colonist, AGGV Archives Scrapbook

101 Doris Leedham Hobbs, "Menelaws Work on Show at Gallery," Saanich News; Ina D.D. Uhthoff, "Art Pioneer Fine Painter," Victoria Daily Colonist, no date

102 Ina D.D. Uhthoff, "'Emery' Exhibition Outstanding," September 25, 1956, Victoria Daily Colonist, AGGV Archives Scrapbook

103 Ina D.D. Uhthoff, "Immense Vitality Strikes Visitor to Zach Studio," October, 1956, Victoria Daily Colonist, AGGV Archives Scrapbook

104 Ina D.D. Uhthoff, "Amess Hand Paints B.C.

in Big Way," February 7, 1957, *Victoria Daily Colonist,* AGGV Archives Scrapbook

105 Ina D.D. Uhthoff, "Experimental Exhibition Draws Splendid Response," July 13, 1957, *Victoria Daily Colonist,* AGGV Archives Scrapbook

106 Ina D.D. Uhthoff, "Island Jury Show Higher in Quality," *Victoria Daily Colonist,* AGGV Archives Scrapbook

107 Ina D.D. Uhthoff, "Yes, It Is a Picture! Painted White on White," June 8, 1957, *Victoria Daily Colonist,* AGGV Archives Scrapbook

108 Ibid.

109 Ina D.D. Uhthoff, "Abstract But Logical," October, 1957, *Victoria Daily Colonist,* AGGV Archives Scrapbook

110 Ina D.D. Uhthoff , "Vigor But No Idea," February 26, 1958, *Victoria Daily Colonist,* AGGV Archives Scrapbook. Artists in the show included Henry Pearson, Cameron Booth, Henry Botkin, Angello Ippolito, Seong Moy, Doris Kriendler, J. von Wieht, K.L. Morris and Arnold Singer.

111 Ina D.D. Uhthoff, "Average Quality Mediocre in New British Paintings," April 6, 1958, *Victoria Daily,* AGGV Archives Scrapbook

112 Ina D.D. Uhthoff, "City Collectors Lend Treasures for Show," September 1956, *Victoria Daily Colonist,* AGGV Archives Scrapbook

113 Ina D.D. Uhthoff, "Vancouver Man's Gift Enriches Collection," March 27, 1957, *Victoria Daily Colonist*

114 Ina D.D. Uhthoff, "Wind, Sand, Sea, Master Artists," *Victoria Daily Colonist,* August 29, 1957, AGGV Archives Scrapbook

115 "Gallery Wing Design Wins Awards," March 16, 1956, Victoria Daily Colonist, AGGV Archives Scrapbook

116 Charles H. Scott and Ian McNairn, *100 Years of B.C. Art,* Vancouver: Vancouver Art Gallery, 1958

CHAPTER SIX: THE LAST DECADE

1 Colin Graham, "Fine Uhthoff Exhibition Calls for Second Look," March 29, 1962, no newspaper cited, Uhthoff Family Collection

2 Arthur Corry, "One Man Show at Gallery Reflects Belief in Nature," April 7, 1962, p. 6, *Victoria Daily Colonist,* Uhthoff Family Collection. Corry found her self-portrait "unflattering to a handsome woman." The photo shows her in a conservative suit with hair carefully coiffed.

3 "Artist Reveals Insight, Skill," July 23, 1963,

Victoria Daily Times, B.C. Archives, Vertical File

4 Ina D.D. Uhthoff, "Barlach Show Tremendous," February 17, 1963, *Victoria Daily Colonist,* AGGV Artist's File

5 Ina D.D. Uhthoff, "Mainland Art 'Alive,'" January 29, 1966, *Victoria Daily Colonist,* AGGV Artist's File

6 Ina D.D. Uhthoff, "Pop Art Restraint Surprising," November 27, (1967?), *Victoria Daily Colonist,* AGGV Archives Scrapbook

7 Ina D.D. Uhthoff, "Women Stimulate December Scene," December 14, 1967, *Victoria Daily Colonist,* AGGV Archives Scrapbook

8 Ibid.

9 Ibid.; Ina D.D. Uhthoff, "Milne's Work Powerful," February 19, 1968, *Victoria Daily Colonist,* expresses her admiration for Milne, AGGV Archives Scrapbook

10 "First Reaction Unappreciative," March 19, 1965, *Victoria Daily Colonist,* Michael Uhthoff Collection

11 Duotang with manuscripts for columns and news clippings, Michael Uhthoff Collection, no date, but most articles are from the 1960s

12 Ina D.D. Uhthoff, "Exhibit Brings Challenge," March 3, 1968, *Victoria Daily Colonist,* AGGV Archives Scrapbook

13 Ina D.D. Uhthoff, "Past Recalled in Collection by Portraitist," no date, no newspaper cited, AGGV Artist File

14 Pat Martin Bates, email to author, November 3, 2011. Ina had apparently wanted Pat and her family to purchase her Constance Avenue home, which Ina "dearly loved."

15 Michael Uhthoff, email to author, January, 2100

16 AGGV *News,* May–June, 1969, Nancy White Collection

17 Nancy Thom White, interview with author, October 23, 2011

18 Nancy White Collection; correspondence from Ina D.D. Uhthoff to Muriel Thom, 1969

19 Nancy White Collection, article about 10 Jenckes Street. It was a Greek Revival style house, built in 1832 as the Leonard Blodget home. Muriel worked as a docent at the Rhode Island School of Design Museum. Though there are some paintings by Muriel, her involvement at the museum was her more notable connection to her mother's world of art.

20 Nancy Thom White interview with author

21 Ibid. Also among Muriel Thom's papers in Nancy

White Collection were articles about parenting, including one by Gloria Steinheim, encouraging parents to take daughters to places where women worked. Growing up with Ina, Muriel would have been aware of this feminist value, especially when she made the effort to complete her physiotherapy degree before marrying.

22 Thom, correspondence to Colin Graham, February 14, 1970, AGGV Exhibition File 1972

23 Ibid.

24 Uhthoff, correspondence to Colin Graham, February 8, 1970, AGGV Exhibition File, 1972. In an undated letter, she outlined her proposal for "Art in Victoria" between 1923–1935 and included pottery, costume design, nature forms in design, crafts, modeling, poster art and colour. "It becomes more interesting as the work develops into the more significant approach to painting." Another undated letter (in which she thanks Colin Graham for his letter of September 27) mentioned photographs of the Victoria School of Art "which I had the temerity to call it." She wanted these photographs on fragile paper handled with care because she had no other record of the early days from 1939 onwards. These photographs have not been located.

25 Ibid. Muriel also wrote that she was glad that her mother's work was safe with the gallery. She wondered whether she could manage an apartment on her own, but knew she was not "nursing home material."

26 Ina Uhthoff, correspondence to Colin Graham, no date, AGGV, 1972 Exhibition File

27 Ibid.

28 "Mystery Object Hovers Over City March 26, 1967; Victoria Daily Colonist; "Mystery Lights Unsolved," "Venus Gave Sky Gazers Run Around," March 27, 1967, Victoria Daily Times in Ina Uhthoff's duotang of news clippings, Michael Uhthoff Collection. Though originally the Dominion Astrophysical Observatory in Saanich was quoted that it could not possibly be Venus, the later article indicated the lights were Venus.

29 Thom, correspondence to Colin Graham, February 14, 1970, AGGV Exhibition File 1972

30 Victoria City and Suburban Directory, 1970

31 "Service Held" February 25, 1971, no newspaper cited, news clipping in Uhthoff Family Collection. His death certificate shows that he was still married and died from cerebral thrombosis in 1971 at 85 at the Kootenay Lake District Hospital in Nelson. John Campbell Uhthoff Family Records on Zip Disk, Uhthoff Family Collection. In an interview October 23, 2011, with Sue Horton (née Docia Jones), she recalled that Ted would visit about once each year and that being around a lot of people got on his nerves.

32 Joy Uhthoff Interview with author

33 "Mrs Uhthoff Dies Suddenly," Carlton Place Newsletter, July 7, 1971, news clipping at B.C. Archives; Paintings, Prints and Drawings Artist File; "Artist's Rites Today," July 1, 1971, Victoria Daily Colonist

34 Graham, Colin Correspondence to John C. Uhthoff, April 25, 1972. After the exhibit, John and his sister Muriel kept in contact with Colin Graham, especially as to how "to relieve the gallery of the burden represented by the collection" [of Ina's works loaned or stored with the gallery]. John sent a cheque to help defer costs. Correspondence John Uhthoff to Colin Graham, June 8, 1973. Later Muriel wrote to Colin about visiting Victoria and alerted him to an upcoming visit to the city by her daughter Fiona who had been working at a visual arts centre in Anchorage, Alaska. "Too bad that Ina is gone. She would have loved to meet Fi in her own territory." Muriel Thom to Colin Graham, April 18, 1977, AGGV Exhibition 1972 File

35 Allen Houghton, "Gallery Glimpses: Gallery Acquiring Ina Uhthoff Collection," The Victorian, April 4, 1973, p. 25

36 Nancy Thom White interview with author, October 23, 2011

37 Colin Graham, Ina D.D. Uhthoff: Memorial Exhibition, Victoria: AGGV, 1972

INDEX

All art by Ina D.D. Uhthoff unless otherwise specified.
Italicized page numbers refer to photos.
An 'n' following a page number refers to an endnote.

*Malakut Reserve at Mill
Bay ferry dock,* (Mount
Tuam, Salt Spring Island
in background), circa
1930s, watercolour
9¾" x 13½"
REPRODUCED FROM
JOHN UHTHOFF'S SLIDES,
JOY/MICHAEL UHTHOFF
COLLECTION